Country Decorating with Fabric

Country Decorating with Fabric

More Than 80 Projects to Add Country Style, Charm & Color to Every Room in Your Home

Chris Rankin

A Sterling/Lark Book
Sterling Publishing Co., Inc.   New York

Editor: Carol Parks

Art Direction and Illustrations: Sandra Montgomery

Translations: Networks, Inc.

Production: Elaine Thompson, Sandra Montgomery

Library of Congress Cataloging-in-Publication Data

Rankin, Chris.

    Country decorating with fabric : more than 80 projects to add country
style, charm, and color to every room in your home / Chris Rankin.

       p. cm.

    "A Sterling/Lark book."

    Includes index.

    ISBN 0-8069-8380-9

    1. House furnishings. 2. Textile fabrics in interior decoration.
3. Decoration and ornament, Rustic. I. Title.

    TT387.R36   1992

    747'.9--dc20   92-3904

                                 CIP

10 9 8 7 6 5 4 3 2 1

A Sterling/Lark Book

First paperback edition published in 1993 by
Sterling Publishing Company, Inc.
387 Park Avenue South, New York, N.Y. 10016

Produced by Altamont Press, Inc.
50 College Street, Asheville, NC 28801

© 1992, Altamont Press

Distributed in Canada by Sterling Publishing
% Canadian Manda Group, P.O. Box 920, Station U
Toronto, Ontario, Canada M8Z 5P9
Distributed in Great Britain and Europe by Cassell PLC
Villiers House, 41/47 Strand, London WC2N 5JE, England
Distributed in Australia by Capricorn Link Ltd.
P.O. Box 665, Lane Cove, NSW 2066

Every effort has been made to ensure that all the information in this book is
accurate. However, due to differing conditions, tools, and individual skills,
the publisher cannot be responsible for any injuries, losses, and other
damages which may result from the use of the information in this book.

Sterling ISBN 0-8069-8380-9 Trade
             0-8069-8381-7 Paper

TABLE OF CONTENTS

INTRODUCTION   6

WORKING WITH FABRIC: THE BASICS   8

LIVING ROOMS   18

KITCHENS & DINING ROOMS   72

BEDROOMS   98

NURSERIES   122

DECORATIVE ACCENTS   132

INDEX OF PROJECTS   160

INDEX   160

INTRODUCTION

.... ✄ ....

A home decorated in the country fashion speaks of comfort, a cheery blend of colors and styles that reflects and adapts to the lives of its inhabitants. These are rooms to be lived in and used, to welcome visitors, and to provide happy surroundings in which to relax at the end of a hard day's work.

Fabric makes it easy to alter the personality of a room with only a small investment of time and money. A few well-placed fabric accessories can soften a room's hard lines, brighten a dark corner, highlight a favorite piece of furniture, or provide a quick change just to celebrate winter's end.

The projects in this book are designed to be fun, and to encourage your own ideas for using fabric in creative ways. Enjoy them!

SELECTING FABRIC

When you choose fabric for a decorating project, there are several factors to consider. First, the fabric should please you. It should be in colors that you like, it should feel good when you touch it, and it should blend with other colors and patterns in the room where it will be used. Most of all, it should suit the way you live. If you are a casual sort of person, you probably won't be happy surrounded by velvet or satin draperies, even though these fabrics look gorgeous in the store. And if you have a job, a family, and several hobbies, you probably don't need the added encumbrance of delicate fabrics that require special care.

Color can completely change the atmosphere of a room. Warm colors can lighten a room on the north side of the house. A pile of pillows in flowery prints may become a focal point in a room that is upholstered and curtained in beige. Soft, cool colors will turn a den into a restful haven.

Where large areas of fabric are used, such as in draperies, and for upholstered pieces that will be with you a long time, you might consider solid colors and more sedate patterns. Use brighter colors and strong patterns for accents, like pillows and lampshades, which you can easily change. If you really do want a wild, exotic print for the couch, then by all means use it!

Fabrics are described both by their fiber content and by their weave, or type of construction. Cotton, wool, silk, and linen are natural fibers. Nylon, polyester, and acrylic are man-made fibers. Rayon, a fiber created from a natural substance, wood pulp, falls somewhere between. Both natural and man-made fibers can be

---

The qualities of a fabric must be considered when planning a project. Every piece of fabric has its own characteristics and its own set of likes and dislikes as far as care and handling are concerned.

---

knitted or woven in a variety of patterns or finishes and are described in these terms too: twill, satin, broadcloth, or damask, for example. Some fabrics, like velvet and corduroy, have a napped finish.

The qualities of a fabric must be considered when planning a project. Every piece of fabric has its own characteristics and its own set of likes and dislikes as far as care and handling are concerned. Natural fiber fabrics are good-looking, have a nice hand

(feel good to the touch), are usually easy to work with, and age gracefully. Cotton is especially easy to sew. Wool has wonderful insulating properties, and silk and linen have a unique beauty no synthetic can equal. Nearly all natural fiber fabrics will shrink to some extent when washed, so should be preshrunk before cutting or should be dry cleaned. Almost all of them *are* washable, if handled with care.

Blends, such as cotton and polyester, may combine the better qualities of both fabrics. They wrinkle less than natural fibers, although they may not be as easy to sew and press. Chlorine bleach can yellow white synthetics. Some, such as nylon, may melt if they come in contact with a very hot surface, and should not be used, for example, for potholders.

If you are not familiar with the qualities of different fabrics, ask a salesperson to help you determine which would be most suitable for your project. Note the care instructions given on the fabric bolt.

Fabrics are of two basic types, decorator and fashion. Decorator fabrics are best for draperies and upholstery. They are heavier and usually 54" to 60" (135 cm to 150 cm) wide. They have a chemical finish that provides stability and sometimes stain resistance. They should be dry cleaned, as washing will remove the finish and change the character of the fabric considerably. Fashion fabrics are intended primarily for clothing construction. They usually are finished less heavily and come in 45" to 54" (115 cm to 135 cm) widths. Many are washable, although some, particularly poor-quality cottons, are heavily finished and will become limp and unstable when washed.

If you are a fabric bargain-hunter, shop carefully. Many fabrics end up in discount stores simply because they are last year's colors or because the manufacturer overproduced. But some are there because they have flaws or defects. Look at your chosen piece carefully as it is unrolled. Be especially wary of off-grain fabrics. The printing and finishing processes can skew the fabric so that it will not hang straight. Fold the piece lengthwise with the selvedge edges together and check that the torn ends are even across the piece. If they are slightly off, the piece probably can be straightened. If they are way out of line, the piece most likely will not straighten, and to use it for a large project, like curtains, would be a disaster.

Watch, too, for off-grain prints. If the fabric is printed with a pattern that produces a crosswise stripe, be sure the stripe is parallel to the torn edges. If not, don't buy it for a large project.

Allow extra yardage for matching stripes, plaids, and prints. Buy extra fabric, too, if the fabric you've chosen is likely to shrink considerably.

The best way to be sure of your fabric choice is to buy a yard and take it home. Wash it the way you'd like to wash the item it will become, test it with fusible interfacing, handle it, sew on it, and see how it looks in its eventual surroundings. If you still love it, go back and buy the rest.

Sewing Room Tools

For the projects in this book you will need just the basic equipment. Good tools make sewing projects faster and easier, and give the best results in the end.

Sewing machine. A simple machine with zigzag stitch capability is all you need. Keep it clean and free of lint, especially around the bobbin hook and around the feed dogs, and oil it as necessary. Above all, use a perfect needle of the type specified in your instruction manual and in a size to suit your fabric. No matter how elaborate your machine, it cannot do a good job with a dull or incorrect needle. It's a good practice to change the needle each time you begin a new sewing project.

You will need a straight stitch/zigzag pressure foot,

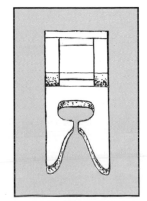

Zigzag Foot

and a zipper foot. Other presser feet will be helpful for certain projects, but are not essential: a cording or piping foot, walking foot or even-feed foot, applique

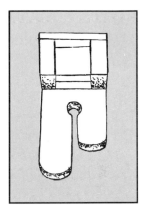

Straight Foot

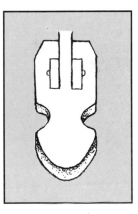

Zipper Foot

foot, blind hem foot, and edge-stitching foot.

Serger. If you own one, you know what a time-saver a serger can be. It, too, needs a frequent change of needles and regular oiling. Sergers produce a great deal of lint, and must be kept clean because lint build-up on the thread guides can interfere with stitch quality. "Canned" air is good for a quick and thorough cleaning.

Scissors. Good scissors allow you to cut fabric cleanly and with ease. Dressmaker's shears with 8" (20 cm) blades are best for general cutting out. Trimming scissors, with short blades and very sharp points, let you cut into small areas and trim close to stitching. Pinking shears provide a ravel-resistant finish for seams. Never, never, *never* use your sewing scissors to cut anything but fabric. And keep them hidden from the children

A *rotary cutter and mat* will speed up many cutting jobs and can be used with a ruler to cut perfectly straight edges. The cutter will go through several layers of fabric at a time, making it especially helpful in cutting pieces for quilting.

Pins. Use good, sharp ones. Pins with glass or plastic heads are easier to see in the fabric—and in the carpet. Throw away dull or bent pins; they can damage delicate fabrics.

A *point turner* will produce sharp, neat corners. Scissors are not a good substitute!

Fabric markers. Many different kinds are available, each useful in certain situations. Test all of them on fabric scraps, and follow the manufacturer's instructions for use. Chalk markers, made of plastic with a small wheel in an opening, dispense powdered chalk in a very fine line. Felt-tip markers come with water-soluble ink or disappearing ink. A waterproof marker is best for drawing on stenciling acetate or for patterns that will be traced onto fabric.

Measuring equipment. Essential are a tape measure, a ruler, preferably of clear plastic for marking straight lines and for cutting with a rotary cutter, and a carpenter's square for producing perfect right angles.

A *cardboard cutting mat* with a printed grid provides a large surface for laying out and cutting,

Cutting Mat

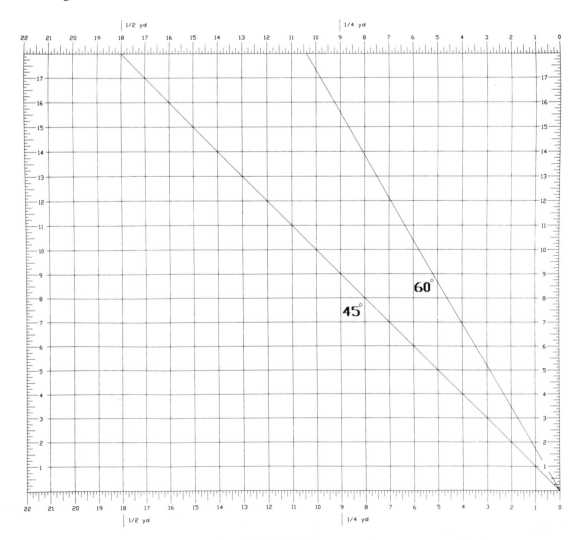

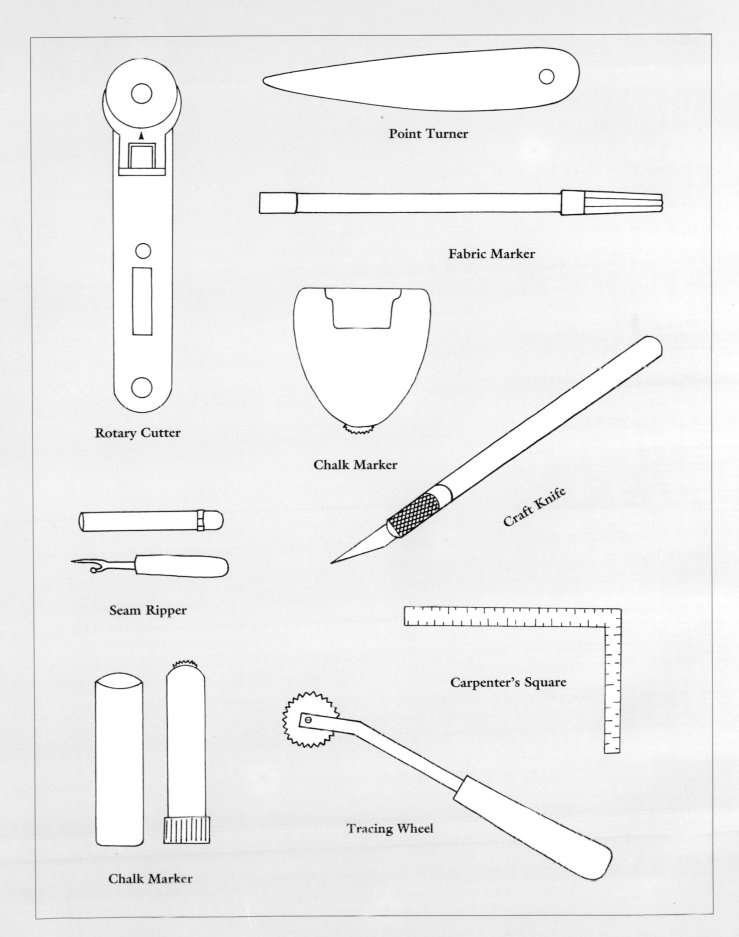

Point Turner

Fabric Marker

Rotary Cutter

Chalk Marker

Craft Knife

Seam Ripper

Carpenter's Square

Chalk Marker

Tracing Wheel

and is helpful for squaring fabric and measuring.

Dressmaker's carbon is used with a tracing wheel for transferring designs to fabric, or for marking cutting lines from a pattern. Test the carbon paper with your fabric to be sure the lines will wash out.

A craft knife is used for cutting applique shapes and stencils. If you use the knife for other materials, be sure the blade is sharp before cutting fabric with it.

Seam ripper. Let's call it a seam improver instead!

A glue stick is useful for holding pieces in position for sewing. Let the glue dry before stitching.

Fabric glue and ***white craft glue*** serve many purposes. They are water soluble and usually will not stain fabrics. Test with each fabric to be sure.

Liquid fray preventer is a permanent edge finish, especially valuable for use on closely clipped corners and with fabrics that ravel easily.

BEHIND·THE·SCENES MATERIALS

The materials that don't show are as important to the look of your finished project as your carefully chosen outer fabric.

Interfacings. There are many kinds of interfacings available, with new ones appearing on the market regularly. All fall into two categories: sew-in and fusible. Both are made of different materials and are of different weights. Ask a salesperson which would best suit your purpose, then test the interfacing with the fabric you plan to use. If you plan to wash an item made with fusible interfacing, first wash a fused sample. Follow the manufacturer's instructions for preshrinking and fusing the interfacing.

Paper-backed transfer web is designed especially for applique work. Follow the manufacturer's instructions for use.

Non-woven pattern drafting material printed with a grid is extremely useful for enlarging patterns to size. It also is good for slipcover and upholstery patternmaking because it is soft enough to be fitted directly onto the furniture piece.

Batting and stuffing. Batting is available by the yard in various widths and thicknesses, or in pieces cut to bedding sizes for quiltmaking. Fiberfill batting will not clump when washed, as cotton batting sometimes does. Loose-pack fiberfill can be used for stuffing pillows and oddly shaped pieces.

Tear-away backing is a stiff, non-woven material used behind machine embroidery to give stability to the fabric.

BEFORE YOU BEGIN

If necessary, straighten the grain of your fabric, especially on large pieces to be used for curtains or bedspreads. Sometimes this can be done by simply pulling the fabric diagonally. If stretching doesn't do the job, fold the piece lengthwise with the selvedges together, machine baste the ends evenly together, then wash the fabric.

Preshrink the fabrics if you plan to wash the finished item. This simply means washing the fabrics the way you will wash the item. If two or more different fabrics will be used in the same piece, preshrinking is especially important, because the fabrics may shrink at different rates. Some fabrics—notably cotton knits and cotton flannel—shrink a great deal and should be washed and dried two or three times before they are cut. Most fabrics will shrink only in length, and little or not at all in width. After it is dry, press the fabric carefully with the lengthwise grain, keeping the fabric straight.

Plan before you cut! Lay out all the pattern pieces on the fabric before you cut the first piece. Cut long pieces on the lengthwise grain, which has less stretch than the crosswise grain. If the fabric has a nap or one-way design, place the tops of all pattern pieces toward one end of the fabric. Carefully match prints, plaids, and stripes where necessary, matching at the seamlines, not at the cutting lines.

A NOTE ABOUT MEASUREMENTS

For all the projects in this book, measurements are given both in inches and in centimeters (or in yards and meters). Anyone who has ever struggled to convert English measurements to metric ones—and vice versa—knows that they simply *don't* convert without resorting to a string of decimal points.

In rounding off measurements, adjustments have necessarily been made to insure accurate fit. Consequently, a measurement given in inches may not be precisely equal to the corresponding measurement in centimeters. For best results, choose one system of measurement—either inches or centimeters—and use it throughout the project.

TECHNIQUES

The projects in this book require only basic sewing skills. A few special techniques are used for some of the projects. If you are not an experienced sewer, take a few minutes to read about these techniques when you begin a project that calls for one of them.

Pressing

Pressing is as important to the look of your project as is sewing—and expert pressing can hide some less-than-perfect sewing. Press each seam after it is sewn, before stitching across it in the next step. First press the line of stitching to merge the stitches with the fabric, then press the seam open or press both seam allowances to one side. Press gently, with the lengthwise grain of the fabric wherever possible.

Reminders

Even an expert occasionally forgets to hold the thread ends at the beginning of a seam. Holding the threads to one side for the

first few stitches will prevent bobbin jams.

If your machine does not have self-adjusting thread tension, set the upper thread tension to suit your fabric.

Use a stitch length that works best for your fabric. A setting of 12 stitches per inch (2.5) works well for many medium-weight fabrics. For thin fabrics, or if the fabric puckers, try a shorter stitch length.

Don't pull your fabric as you sew; let the feed dogs do the work.

Tailor's Knot

Backstitch the ends of seams to secure them by sewing back and forth several times over 1/2" (1.5 cm) of the stitching line. If the ends of the stitching line will remain exposed, tie a tailor's knot. Pull on the bobbin thread to pull a loop of the top thread to the wrong side, then pull the thread end through. Tie a loose knot with both threads. Slip a needle through the knot, place the point just at the end of the stitching line, and slowly tighten the knot, at the same time slipping it down the needle tightly against the fabric.

Corners

Here's how to make a perfect corner. On the wrong side, mark the point at the corner where the seamlines intersect. Stitch to within about 3/4" (2 cm) of the

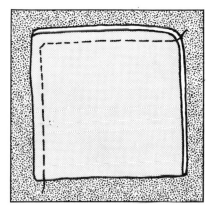

Shortened Stitches and One Diagonal Stitch

mark, then shorten the stitch length. Sew almost to the mark and pivot, with the needle down in the fabric; take one stitch on the diagonal, and pivot again. Sew 3/4" or so, return the stitch length to normal. The diagonal stitch makes a neater corner when the piece is turned right side out. For heavy fabric, take two diagonal stitches at the corner. Trim the fabric close to the stitching across the corner, tapering to a wider seam allowance along the straight edges. A dab of liquid fray preventer at the corner will keep it from pulling out.

Curved Seams

For outer curves, sew the seam, then cut notches in the seam allowance to within about 1/8" (4 mm) of the stitching line at 1/2" (1.5 cm) intervals. The piece will lie flat after it's turned. For inner curves, clip at regular intervals to 1/8" (4 mm) from the stitching line. If the fabric is loosely woven or tends to ravel, stay stitch the curves before sewing the seam:

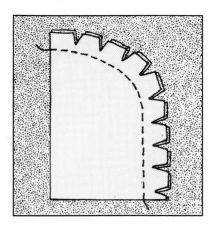

Notching a Curved Seam

sew a line of straight stitch 1/8" (4 mm) inside the seamline. Clip or notch to the stay stitching after sewing the seam. When sewing a curved piece to a straight piece, stay stitch the curved piece and clip it as above, before sewing, to make it easier to fit the pieces together.

Finishing Seams

Seams should be finished neatly if they will be seen, or to prevent fraying if the piece will be washed. A serger will do the job quickly, but most sewing machines also are equipped with good overcast stitches. Even a simple zigzag stitch does a fine job of seam finishing.

The seam allowances can be overcast separately, or you can overcast them together if the fabric is not too thick. For all overcast stitches, position the fabric so the needle goes just over the fabric edge on the right swing.

If the pieces were cut on the fabric selvedge, finishing is not necessary, but do clip through the selvedge at intervals of about

1" (3 cm), because the selvedge may shrink more than the fabric itself when the piece is washed.

Piping

Piping is a professional touch and adds a finished look to many projects, especially upholstery—*if* it is made well. Piping is not difficult to do if the instructions are followed carefully.

Strips of fabric for piping can be cut on the straight grain of the fabric if the piping is to be sewn primarily to straight edges. If it will be used around curves and corners, it will be easier to fit if the fabric strips are cut on the bias. In either case, it usually will be necessary to piece strips together to get the required length. Sew bias strips together along the fabric grainline, as shown.

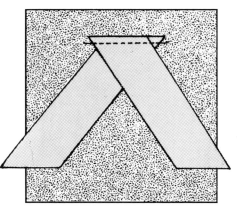

**Sewing Bias Strips
Along the Grainline**

When measuring for piping, allow about 1" (3 cm) extra for each outer corner and for each end. Cut a length of cord slightly longer than the fabric strip. Fold the strip in half lengthwise, right side out, and press the cord firmly into the fold. Using a piping or cording foot, or a zipper foot, stitch the fabric together as

closely to the cord as possible. Take care not to pull the fabric, as this will cause wrinkles in the finished piping. Trim the seam allowances so they are the width of the seam allowances on the piece to which the piping will be sewn.

Sew the piping to the right side of one fabric piece, matching raw edges and seamlines. Stitch to the piece, sewing on the piping stitching line. Cut notches in the seam allowance to the stitching line to go around outer corners, at about 1/4" (.5 cm) intervals for

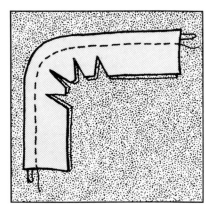

Notching for Outer Corners

a right-angle corner, or farther apart for a curve. Clip to the stitching line to sew around inner curves, as for sewing

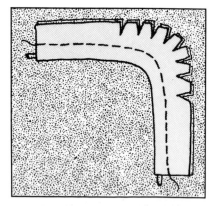

Notching for Inner Corners

curved seams. If the piped seam ends at another seamline, sew the piping all the way to the edge of the fabric. If, for example, it is placed around a cushion, stitch both ends into the seam at the point where they meet.

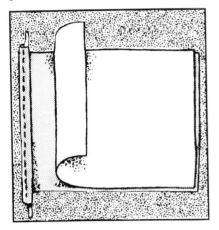

The Piped Piece and the Second Fabric Piece

Sew the piped piece to the second fabric piece with right sides together and the piping sandwiches between them. Sew along the previous stitching line.

Zippers

A zipper in a cushion cover allows you to remove the cover for laundering or dry cleaning, and gives a neat appearance to the back of the cushion. A zipper can be sewn centered over the

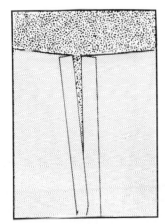

Machine baste the seam closed.

seam, or lapped to cover the zipper completely. For either method, machine baste the portion of the seam in which the zipper will be inserted, allowing an extra 1/2" (1.5 cm) at the top of the zipper. Press the seam open. Press the zipper tapes. If the zipper will be inserted in the center of a longer seam rather than at an end, as on the back of a pillow, whipstitch the upper ends of the tape together. Use a zipper foot for all sewing.

Centered application. Fold back one side of the seam allowance. Open the zipper and place it face down against the wrong side of the seam allowance, with the stop

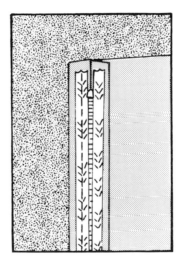

Baste the second tape to the seam allowance.

at the bottom of the basted seam and the excess basted seam at the top of the zipper. Place the zipper teeth just next to the seamline. Baste. Stitch one side of the tape to the seam allowance only, stitching about 1/8" (4 mm) from the teeth. Close the zipper. Baste the other side of the tape to the other seam allowance; stitch.

On the outside, mark the lower

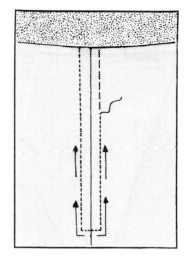

Sew the zipper from the outside.

end of the zipper. Start at that point, stitch across the bottom and up one side, 1/4" to 3/8" (.5 cm to 1 cm) from the center seamline. Sew to 1/2" (1.5 cm) above the pull. Repeat for the other side, sewing in the same direction. If the zipper is in the center of a longer seam, sew across the upper end as well.

Lapped application. Extend one seam allowance (the underlapping side). Open the zipper and place face down on the wrong side of the seam allowance, with the teeth just next to the seamline. Baste, then stitch, through the seam allowance only, stitching 3/16" (5 mm) from the teeth.

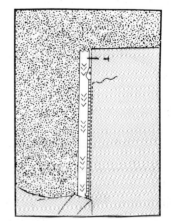

Stitch one tape to the seam allowance.

15

Turn the zipper face up, folding the fabric but keeping the zipper tape flat. Keep the fold about 1/8" (4 mm) from the teeth. Lay the piece flat. Close the zipper and turn face down over the free seam allowance. Pleats will form at the ends of the zipper. Secure at the ends with pins.

On the outside, stitch across the lower end and up the unstitched side. If the zipper is in the center of a seam, stitch across the top as well, about 1/2" (1.5 cm) above the pull.

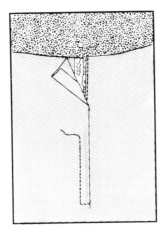

Stitch across the lower end and up the side.

Hems

If a hem will be visible or if the finished item is to be washed, use double hems to finish edges. Turn the raw edge of the fabric to the wrong side, according to the measurements specified in the directions for the project, and press the fold. Then turn under the raw edge again, evenly, and press this fold. If the hem is fairly wide, make the second fold about 1/2" (1.5 cm). If the hem is narrow, make the second fold narrower too. If the directions simply call for a narrow double hem, turn under the edge about 1/4"

(.75 cm) the first time, and make the second fold so that the raw edge meets the first foldline. Always press the folds before stitching.

A single hem is sufficient if the hem will not show, and if the item will be dry cleaned. For a single hem, just turn under the edge one time, to the measurement specified in the project directions.

If your machine has a blind hem stitch, follow the instructions in your manual for its use. The machine blind hem is a quick way to finish large pieces neatly.

Edgestitching and Topstitching

Both terms refer simply to lines of stitching that show on the outside. Topstitching is usually about 1/4" (1 cm) from an edge or seam, and edgestitching is very close to the edge or seamline. A neat line of topstitching adds a finished, professional look to a project, and when it is sewed through one or both seam allowances it also serves to strengthen the seam.

Stitching a straight line is *not* difficult. It's much like driving a car in a straight line—easier to accomplish if you look at a point ahead, rather than at the place where you are. Stitching tends to be straighter if you don't sew too slowly. For neat corners, mark turning points where the seamlines intersect, then pivot at the marks with the needle down in the fabric.

Applique

This is a good technique for making use of favorite design motifs, for repeating a motif from anoth-

er fabric in the room, for adding color, or for personalizing a gift.

Fuse interfacing or paper-backed transfer web to the fabric pieces from which you will cut the applique motifs, following the manufacturer's instructions. This will give stability to the pieces and prevent distortion of the shapes during sewing.

Draw or trace the design on the interfaced side of the fabric.

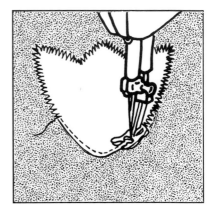

Applique with a zigzag stitch.

Remember to place the tracing or pattern upside down, so the design will be right side up on the right side of the fabric. Use dressmakers' carbon to trace, or watersoluble marker to draw a design.

Cut the shapes from the fused fabric. If paper-backed transfer web is used, remove the backing and fuse the appliques to the right side of the main fabric. For other kinds of fusible interfacing, dot the pieces with a glue stick to hold them in place while sewing.

Stitch the applique with an applique foot or a machine embroidery foot. Use a zigzag stitch with a fairly short stitch length, making the stitches close together. Use a medium stitch width. The stitching should just cover the raw edge of the applique.

If the applique was not fused in place, first sew the applique to the main fabric with a row of straight stitch, stitching all around the piece about 1/8" (4 mm) from the edge. Then zigzag around the edge, covering both the edge of the applique piece and the row of straight stitch.

To turn a sharp corner, sew all the way to the center, and stop with the needle in the fabric on the right swing. Pivot, and over-sew the first line of stitching squarely at the corner.

Quilting

Quilting can be functional, pro-viding insulation in a tea cozy or bedspread, or it can be purely decorative, giving texture and dimension to a plain piece of fab-ric. Quilting need not be just par-allel rows of straight stitching. Try quilting around a motif in a print fabric, or try quilting with one of your machine's simple decorative stitches.

Mark quilting lines on the right side of one fabric piece with a fabric marker. Place the pieces to be quilted with wrong sides together and the batting between them. If the fabric layers don't feed evenly during sewing, use a walking foot or even-feed foot, or reduce presser foot pressure slightly.

Gathering

Gathered ruffles at the edges of curtains or around chair cush-ions will give a softer look to a room.

Lengthen upper thread tension by one number. Set stitch length at about 8 stitches per inch (3.5).

On the *right* side, stitch 2 rows, one on either side of the seamline and about 1/4" (1 cm) apart. Leave long thread tails at both ends of the stitching. For a long piece, break the stitching at intervals—both stitching lines at the same point—to avoid having gathering threads so long that they may break when it is drawn up. Mark centers on the piece to be gathered and on the piece to which it will be sewn. Draw up both bobbin threads to gather the piece to fit, matching marks at centers. Allow extra fullness at

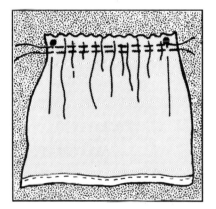

Gathering a Short Piece

corners. Place a pin at each end of the line of gathering, and secure the threads by wrapping them in a figure 8 around the pins. Gather the piece to a length slightly shorter than the piece to which it attaches, as the gathered piece will lengthen slightly when sewn.

Sew the pieces together, stitching halfway between the gathering lines. Press just from the edge to the seamline. Remove the gathering thread outside the seamline by pulling out the bob-bin thread.

To gather a very long piece, such as a dust ruffle, place a

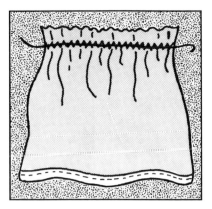

Gathering a Long Piece

length of thin cord or heavy thread inside the seamline. Sew the end of the cord securely in place. Stitch over the cord with an open zigzag stitch, just inside the seamline, taking care not to sew through the cord. Then draw up the cord to gather.

Stenciling

Stenciling is an easy way to apply your own designs to fabric. Many different kinds of fabric paint are available in craft supply stores. Always test the paint on your fab-ric. If you plan to wash the sten-ciled item, paint a sample piece and wash it before proceeding with your project. Follow the manufacturer's instructions for setting the paint after it has dried.

Trace your design on the sten-ciling acetate with a waterproof marker or with dressmakers' car-bon and cut out the design areas. Position the stencil on the fabric.

Use a stenciling brush. Wipe off excess paint so that you are painting with a fairly dry brush. Hold the brush vertically, and dab the paint onto the fabric, taking care that paint doesn't run under the edges of the acetate.

CONTEMPORARY COUNTRY ROOM

.... ℘ ....

Cauntry style is a spacious concept, with room for a variety of looks. It can mean a cozy country den with checked fabric, painted surfaces, and lots of bric-a-brac. But it can also encompass a sparer, leaner, more modern look, implying rich bare wood complemented by carefully placed fabric accents.

This contemporary country room is the second type. Although the fabric is patterned and striped, the colors are fairly subdued and the feeling is restrained—even for the patchwork duck (page 20). Other projects in the room are striped and floral pillows (page 23), classic fabric-covered boxes (page 24), and picture mats (page 25). Since many living rooms also include dining areas, there are matching napkins and tablecloth (page 26) and a teapot "soft sculpture" (page 27). To complete the room, there's a fabric-covered vase (page 30) and a smartly checked lampshade (page 31).

PATCHWORK DUCK

〜

• **MATERIALS**

Small pieces of fabric in assorted cotton prints, small pieces of dark green cotton, matching thread, white embroidery floss, fiberfill, ribbon or strip of fabric 12" (30 cm) long.

• **INSTRUCTIONS**

Make full-size paper patterns for all pieces. From doubled fabric, cut wings, head, lower body, and side/back pieces with no seam allowance added. Add 1/4" (1 cm) seam allowance and cut the lower beak from a single thickness of fabric and the upper beak from double thickness. From dark green cotton, cut 2 circles 1/4" (1 cm) in diameter for eyes, and 2 strips 1/8" x 1/4" (.5 cm x 1 cm) for nostrils.

Sew all pieces with right sides together and with 1/4" (1 cm) seam allowance. Use a short stitch length.

Position the eye circles on the head and applique in place, using a close zigzag stitch. Sew the nostrils to the upper beak pieces in the same way. By hand, make 2 horizontal satin stitches on each eye, using 3 strands of white floss.

Sew the head pieces together. Sew the beak together and turn right side out. Sew beak to head with right sides together; turn. Stuff the beak and the head, packing the fiberfill tightly.

Sew the body pieces together, using the photo as a guide. Turn right side out and stuff. Sew head to the body by hand, folding under the seam allowance. Tie ribbon around the neck to cover the seamline. ∎

Patchwork Duck Pattern

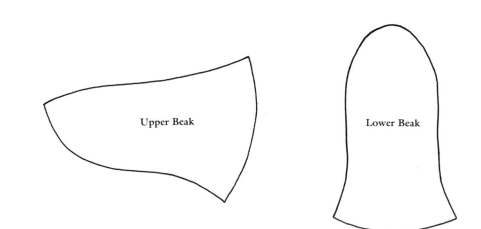

Upper Beak

Lower Beak

Patchwork Duck Pattern (cont.)

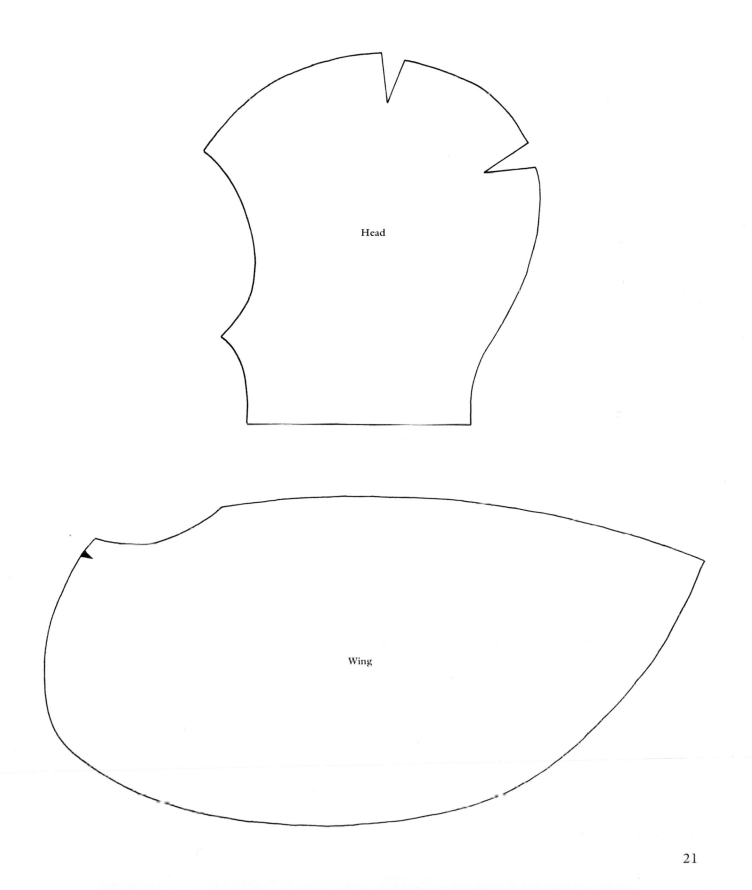

Head

Wing

Patchwork Duck Pattern (cont.)

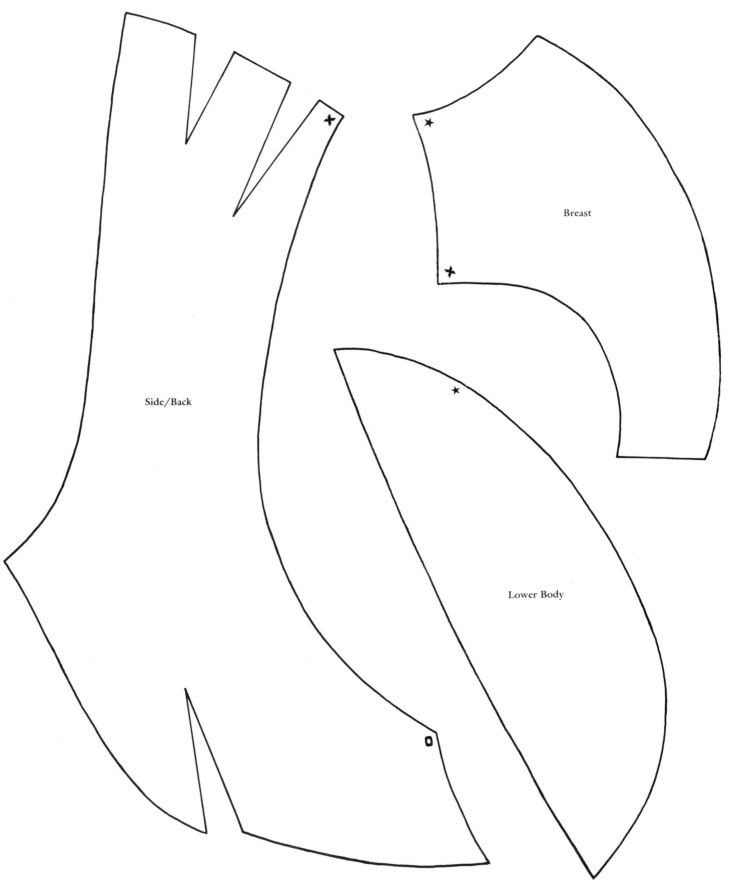

Side/Back

Breast

Lower Body

STRIPED AND FLORAL PILLOWS

∽

• **MATERIALS**

For each pillow: floral print or 2 coordinating striped fabrics, thread, 1-1/2 yds (1.2 m) double fold bias tape 1/2" (1.5 cm) wide, pillow form.

• **INSTRUCTIONS**

FLORAL PILLOW

Measure the length and width of the pillow form. Cut fabric for front to this measurement plus 1/2" (1.5 cm) seam allowance on all sides. Cut back the same, but add 1-1/2" (4 cm) at one side (for a rectangular pillow, extend one of the narrow ends). Cut the back in half at center, widthwise. Place the halves with right sides together and make a 3/4" (2 cm) seam, leaving an opening at the center large enough to insert the pillow form. Hem the seam allowances along the opening with double hems. Cut the bias tape into 4 strips and sew 2 to each side of the opening opposite each other. Stitch the front to the back with right sides together around all edges. Clip corners and turn right side out. Insert the form and tie the ties.

BORDERED PILLOW

Work the same as for the floral pillows, but add 3" (7.5 cm) seam allowance instead of 1/2" (1.5 cm) around all edges. After cover is turned right side out, stitch 2-1/2" (6 cm) inside the edges on all sides with a medium zigzag stitch to shape the border.

STRIPED PILLOW

Measure the length and width of the pillow form. From one striped fabric, cut 2 pieces to the above measurements plus 1/2" (1.5 cm) seam allowance on all sides. Cut a strip of the second striped fabric 6" (15 cm) wide and twice the length of the form plus 1" (3 cm). For the ties, cut 4 or 6 strips of the second fabric 1-1/4" x 12" (3 cm x 30 cm).

Sew the 2 large pieces of fabric around 3 sides with right sides together, with 1/2" (1.5 cm) seam allowance. Clip corners and turn right side out. With right sides together, sew the narrow ends of the strip with 1/2" (1.5 cm) seam allowance. Make a 1/2" (1.5 cm) single hem around one edge of the strip. Sew the unhemmed edge of the strip to the open edge of the cover with right sides together. Turn the flap to the inside of the cover; press.

For the ties, fold the strips in half lengthwise, right sides together, and stitch long edge and one end of each with 1/4" (1 cm) seam allowance. Turn right side out. Turn under open ends; press. Pin the ties, opposite each other in pairs, to the inner edge of the cover, with the tie ends extending 1/2" (1.5 cm) into the cover. Stitch all around the seamed edge of the cover, 1/4" (1 cm) from the edge, stitching tie ends in place. Insert pillow form and arrange inner flap to cover form. ∎

FABRIC-COVERED BOXES

∽

• MATERIALS

Round boxes with lids, cotton print fabric, white glue, medium-weight fusible interfacing, scissors, pencil, ruler.

• INSTRUCTIONS

Lay the fabric wrong side up on a table and place the box on the fabric. Draw around the bottom of the box. Add 1/2" (1.5 cm) around the outside of the circle and cut from the fabric. Cut a fabric strip to fit around the outside of the box, adding 1" (3 cm) to the height. Fuse interfacing to the wrong sides of both pieces.

Spread glue evenly over the bottom of the box and center the box on the wrong side of the fabric circle. Clip small notches in the fabric to the edge of the box, about 1" (3 cm) apart, all around the circle. Spread glue around the lower 1/2" (1.5 cm) of the box and glue the bottom seam allowance to the sides of the box.

Press under top and bottom edges of the fabric strip so piece is exactly the height of the box. Glue hems in place. Spread glue evenly around the outside of the box and glue fabric to it.

Cover the lid of the box in the same way. Allow glue to dry completely before placing top on the box. ■

FLORAL PICTURE MATS

∽

• **MATERIALS**

Floral print cotton fabric, mat board, picture frame, cardboard, ruler, craft knife, pencil, white glue.

• **INSTRUCTIONS**

Cut rectangle from mat board to fit inside frame. Mark an inner rectangle 2-1/2" (6 cm) inside edges of the mat. Cut out the inner rectangle. Place mat on wrong side of fabric. Draw around inner and outer edges of mat. Add 1" (3 cm) around inner and outer edges of mat outline and cut fabric on these lines.

Spread glue evenly on one side and around all edges of mat. Press fabric in place. Clip fabric diagonally to corners of the mat. Spread glue along edges on the back of the mat. Fold fabric to back and press in place.

Position picture against back of the mat. Back the picture with cardboard cut to the same size as the mat, and set in the frame. ∎

BORDERED TABLECLOTH AND MATCHING NAPKINS

෫

• FINISHED MEASUREMENTS

Tablecloth, 55" (140 cm) square. Napkins, 18" (45 cm) square.

• MATERIALS

TABLECLOTH

3/4 yd (.7 m) cotton print fabric 56" (140 cm) wide. 1-1/2 yds (1.4 m) cotton fabric in a complementary print, 56" (140 cm) wide. 5-1/4 yds (4.7 m) double fold bias tape 3/4" (2 cm) wide, thread.

NAPKINS

Cotton print fabric 18" (45 cm) square, 2-1/8 yds (2 m) double fold bias tape 1/2" (1.5 cm) wide in same color as for tablecloth, thread.

• INSTRUCTIONS

TABLECLOTH

Cut the 3/4 yd (.7 m) piece of fabric into 4 strips 6-1/4" x 56" (16 cm x 140 cm). With right sides together, sew the strip ends at 45-degree angles with 1/4" (1 cm) seams to form a hollow square.

From the other print fabric cut a 46-1/4" (116 cm) square. Pin the solid square right side up onto the right side of the hollow square with raw edges evenly overlapped. Stitch the pieces together on the right side, close to the edges of the solid square. On the wrong side of the cloth, turn under the inner raw edge of the hollow square 1" (3 cm) toward the *right side* of the fabric, clipping diagonally at corners. Press.

Press open the center lengthwise fold of the bias tape. Beginning at the center of one side on the right side of the cloth, pin tape over the stitching line. Make tucks to miter corners. Stitch both edges of tape to the cloth, folding under the overlapping end. Stitch a 1/2" (1.5 cm) double hem around outer edges.

NAPKINS

Fold seam binding over the edges and stitch in place. Make small pleats to miter corners, and fold under the overlapping end. ■

TEAPOT SOFT SCULPTURE

∾

- **FINISHED MEASUREMENTS**

8-3/4" (22 cm) diameter.

- **MATERIALS**

1 yd (.8 m) floral print fabric 56" (140 cm) wide, checked fabric 8" x 20" (20 cm x 51 cm), thread, medium thickness fiberfill batting 22" x 26" (55 cm x 65 cm), loose pack fiberfill, heavy cardboard, white glue.

- **INSTRUCTIONS**

Make full-size paper patterns for all pieces. From batting, cut 6 body pieces, adding 1/4" (1 cm) seam allowance only at top and bottom edges. With floral fabric doubled and with 1/4" (1 cm) seam allowance added to all pieces, cut the body piece 6 times, and the handle and spout pieces once. Cut 2 circles 7" (18 cm) in diameter. From the checked fabric cut 1 circle 7-3/4" (19 cm) in diameter, and 2 circles 5" (12.5 cm) in diameter. Cut a cardboard circle 4" (10.5 cm) in diameter, and another 5" (12.5 cm) in diameter. Sew all pieces with right sides together and with 1/4" (1 cm) seam allowance.

For the outside of the teapot, sew 6 body pieces together along the long edges to form a cylinder. Machine baste around the lower edge (the larger opening) at the seamline. Sew

the batting pieces, abutting the long edges and stitching together with a zigzag stitch. Sew the other 6 body pieces together along the long edges for the lining. Stitch the batting to the wrong side of the lining around the upper edge, inside the seamline. Machine baste together around the lower edge, on the seamline.

Draw up the basting thread at the lower edge of the outer teapot to fit the floral circle. Stitch one circle to the bottom of the teapot.

With the lining to the outside of the outer pot and right sides together, machine baste lining to outer pot along the upper seamline. Gather to a diameter of 4" (10 cm) and stitch over gathering line. Trim batting close to stitching, trim seam allowances to 1/8" (.5 cm), and turn lining to inside. Draw up basting thread at bottom of lining to fit bottom of pot.

With a long stitch, sew around the remaining floral circle 1/2" (1.5

cm) inside the edge. Place the larger cardboard circle on the wrong side of the fabric circle and draw up the basting thread to fold edges of the fabric over the cardboard. Glue edges to the cardboard. Place the covered circle, right side up, inside the pot. Hand stitch to the bottom of the pot.

Sew the handle pieces together, leaving ends open. Turn right side out and stuff with fiberfill. Hand stitch to the pot about 2" (5 cm) above the lower edge, turning under raw edges. Sew the spout pieces together, leaving the lower end open. Turn, stuff, and sew to the pot opposite the handle, about 4-3/4" (12 cm) above the lower edge.

For the lid, mark a circle 2-1/2" (6 cm) in diameter in the center of the larger checked circle and machine baste around it. Place a handful of fiberfill in the inner circle, on the wrong side, and place the remaining cardboard circle over it. Draw up the basting thread to fold the edges of the fabric over the cardboard, and glue edges in place. Sew around one of the small checked circles, 1/2" (1.5 cm) inside the edge, with a long stitch. Draw up the basting thread slightly, fold edges to wrong side, and press. Hand stitch to the underside of the lid.

For the lid pot, machine baste around the remaining checked circle, 1/2" (1.5 cm) inside the edge. Place a handful of fiberfill on the wrong side and draw up the basting thread tightly. Hand stitch securely and stitch knob to top of lid. ■

Teapot Pattern

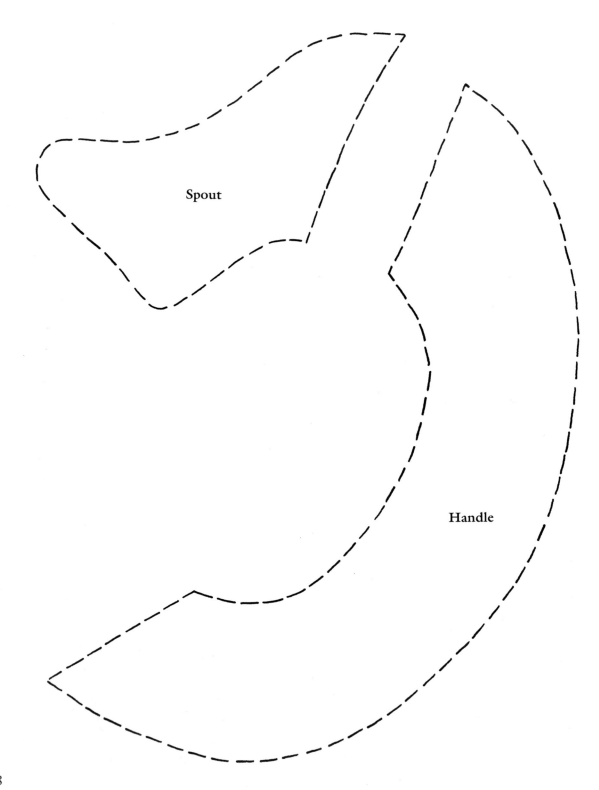

Spout

Handle

Teapot Pattern (cont.)

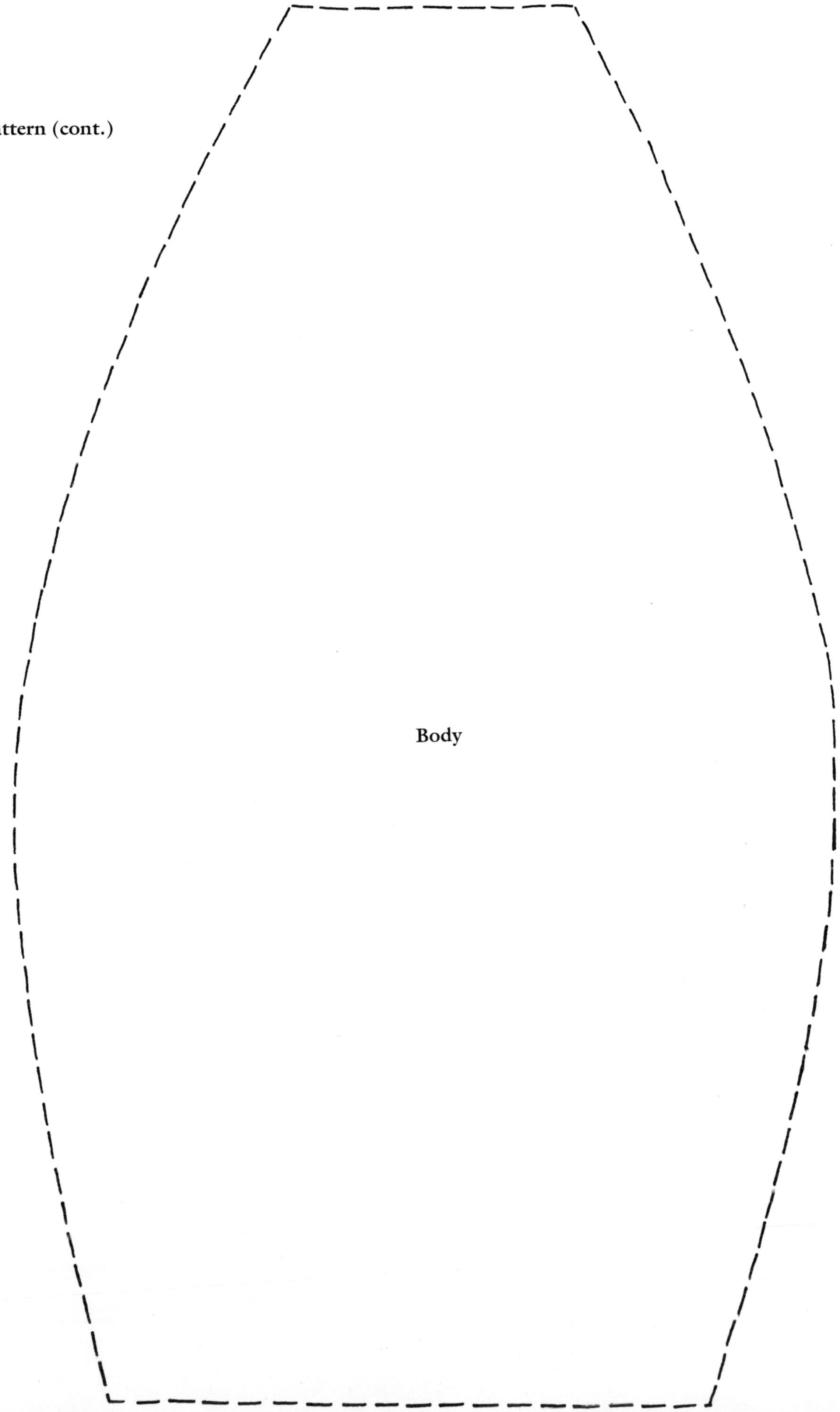

Body

FABRIC-COVERED VASE

∽

• MATERIALS

A vase, cotton print fabric, ribbon, rubber band.

• INSTRUCTIONS

Place the fabric on a table, wrong side up. Place a rubber band around the neck of the vase. Set the vase at the center of the fabric and fold the fabric up around it. Tuck the ends of the fabric under the rubber band. Tie a ribbon around the neck of the vase. ■

CHECKED LAMPSHADE

∽

• MATERIALS

Lampshade form, checked cotton fabric, double fold bias tape 3/4" (2 cm) wide, white glue, lightweight white glossy card stock, paper, thread, pencil.

• INSTRUCTIONS

Make a paper pattern of the form. Roll the form along the paper, marking the beginning and ending points and drawing along the upper and lower edges. Cut this piece from card stock. Add 1/2" (1.5 cm) seam allowance around all edges of the pattern and cut from the fabric. Cut 2 strips of paper 3/4" (2 cm) wide and the height of the pattern.

Roll the card stock into a conical shape, abutting the ends. Glue the paper strips over the seam on the inside and outside of the cone, securing them with paper clips until the glue dries.

Cut a strip of bias tape the length of the top circumference of the form. Place the fold of the tape over the top of the form and stitch in place all around. Tape around the bottom of the form in the same way.

Spread glue evenly over the outside of the cone and glue the fabric in place, taking care not to stretch the fabric. Place the cone over the form. Fold the upper and lower edges of the fabric over the top and bottom of the form and glue in place. Stitch to the bias binding. ■

ORANGE CHECKED COUNTRY ROOM

·········· ᔰ ··········

V ibrant colors can fill a room—and the people in it—with energy and cheer. Although the same fabric is used throughout this living room, for a well-unified look, any of the individual projects could provide a lively accent for another room. There's a broad hassock and decorative picture mats (page 34), a cushion for a wicker chair (page 35), floor-length drapes and crisscrossed pillows (page 36), and fringed napkins for an informal dining area (page 37).

HASSOCK WITH CHECKED COVER

≈

(See photo on page 32.)

• FINISHED MEASUREMENTS
17-1/2" (44 cm) square, 16" (40 cm) high.

• MATERIALS
1-5/8 yds (1.5 m) each of orange checked cotton fabric and solid orange cotton chintz or broadcloth, 45" (115 cm) wide. 2 pieces of foam rubber 17-1/2" (44 cm) square and 6" (15 cm) thick, one piece of foam rubber 17-1/2" (44 cm) square and 4" (10 cm) thick. 2-1/4 yds (2 m) thick piping cord, thread to match fabric, nylon thread, 2 shank buttons 3/4" (7 cm) in diameter, large upholstery needle with sharp point.

• INSTRUCTIONS
A foam rubber block is covered with solid orange fabric then topped with an orange checked slipcover.

To cover the block, cut from the solid orange fabric 4 pieces 18-1/2" x 17" (46 cm x 43 cm) for the sides, and 2 pieces 18-1/2" (46 cm) square for the top and bottom. From checked fabric cut 5 pieces 18-1/2" (46 cm) square for the top and sides. Also from the checked fabric cut strips 2-3/4" (7 cm) wide and piece them as necessary to form a single strip 80" (203 cm) long.

Sew all pieces with right sides together and with 1/2" (1.5 cm) seam allowance. Sew 3 of the solid orange side pieces together, leaving seams open 1/2" (1.5 cm) from upper and lower edges. Sew the top to 2 adjacent seamed sides. Sew the bottom to the same 2 sides. Stack

the foam blocks and place them in the cover. Hand stitch the remaining seams snugly, beginning with the side seam and turning seam allowances to the inside.

Place one button at center top of the block, and one at center bottom. With doubled nylon thread and the upholstery needle, sew the 2 buttons together through the foam blocks. Wrap the thread securely around the shank of each button.

Fold the long checked strip tightly around the piping cord, right side out. With raw edges together, stitch as closely as possible to the cord, using a piping foot or zipper foot. Trim the seam allowances to 1/2" (1.5 cm). Place the checked top piece right side up and pin the piping around the edges. Begin at a corner, and sew both ends into the seam. Keep raw edges together and clip piping seam allowance to the seamline at the corners. Stitch along the previous stitching line.

Sew the 4 checked side pieces together, ending seams 1/2" (1.5 cm) from the upper edge and 8" (20 cm) from the lower edge. Stitch 1/2" (1.5 cm) double hems in the seam allowances of the openings. Sew top to sides, matching the corners. Trim corners and turn right side out. Stitch a 2" (5 cm) double hem around the bottom. Place cover over the hassock. ■

CHECKED PICTURE MAT

≈

(See photo on page 32.)

• MATERIALS
Rectangular frame, orange checked cotton fabric 2" (5 cm) larger than

inner frame dimensions, white glue, craft knife.

• INSTRUCTIONS
Cut cardboard to fit in the frame. Cut a rectangle from the center of the cardboard, leaving a border about 2-1/2" (6 cm) wide. Center the cardboard on the fabric and outline the outer and inner edges of the rectangle. Spread glue thinly over one side of the cardboard and around the outer edges. Place on the fabric within the outline and press in place. Cut a diagonal X through the fabric in the inner rectangle, stopping the cut 1/8" (3 mm) from the corners of the cardboard. Glue fabric over the inner edges. Trim away excess fabric around all edges. Place the mat in the frame and center needlework or picture behind it. ■

Cut a diagonal X through the fabric in the inner rectangle.

Trim excess fabric from around inner and outer rectangles.

CHECKED CHAIR CUSHION

∽

• MATERIALS

Orange checked cotton fabric, foam rubber 2-1/2" (6 cm) thick, zipper 22" (55 cm) long, 8 shank buttons 3/4" (2 cm) in diameter, thick piping cord, thread to match fabric, nylon thread, sharp upholstery needle.

• INSTRUCTIONS

Make a paper pattern to exactly fit the chair seat. Cut the foam from the pattern. Measure the circumference of the pattern precisely and cut 2 pieces of piping cord this measurement plus 3" (8 cm). Cut 2 pieces of fabric from the pattern, adding 1/2" (1.5 cm) seam allowance around the edges. For piping, cut strips 2-3/4" (7 cm) wide and piece as necessary to form 2 strips the length of the cord. For the side/front edge, cut one piece 3-1/2" (9 cm) wide and the length of the circumference measurement minus 22" (56 cm). For the back edge cut 2 pieces 2-1/4" (6 cm) x 24" (60 cm). Sew all pieces with right sides together and with 1/2" (1.5 cm) seam allowance.

Fold a piping strip tightly around the cord, right side out. With raw edges together, stitch as closely as possible to the cord, using a piping foot or zipper foot. Trim the seam allowances to 1/2" (1.5 cm). Place a cushion piece right side up and pin the piping around the edges, beginning and ending at a back corner and keeping raw edges together. Clip piping seam allowance to the seamline at corners. Stitch along the previous stitching line, sewing ends of the piping into the seams. Repeat with the other cushion piece and piping strip.

Place the back edge pieces with right sides together. On one long edge, stitch 1/2" (1.5 cm) in from each end with short stitches, then baste the remainder of the seam. Press seam open. Center the zipper, wrong side up, over the wrong side of the basted seam and stitch in place. Remove basting. Sew the ends of the back edge to the ends of the side/front edge piece to form a ring.

Sew the cushion top and bottom to the edge piece. Clip seam allowances and turn right side out.

Mark placement for 4 buttons on the cushion top, spacing them evenly around the cushion, 3-1/2" to 5" (9 cm to 13 cm) from the edge. Mark placement points on the bottom of the cushion directly below those on top. With doubled nylon thread and the upholstery needle, sew each pair of buttons together through the foam. Wrap thread securely around the shank of each button. ■

CHECKED CURTAINS

❦

• MATERIALS

Orange checked cotton fabric, curtain rod with end knobs, curtain rings.

• INSTRUCTIONS

Measure across the window and frame. For each curtain, allow 1-1/2 to 2 times half this width for pleats, and 2-1/2" (6 cm) to each for side hems. For the length, measure from the top of the rod to the floor (or desired length), subtract the width of the rings, and add 8" (20 cm) for hems.

When cutting the fabric, match the check pattern across the pair of curtains and allow for a complete check pattern vertically where the curtains will meet at center.

Stitch a 1-1/4" (3 cm) double hem along each side. Hem the upper edges with 2-1/2" (6 cm) double hems and the lower edges with 5-1/2" (14 cm) double hems. Sew rings to the tops of the curtains, beginning at the sides and spacing the rings evenly at about 4" (10 cm) intervals across the curtains. ■

CRISSCROSSED PILLOWS

❦

(See photo on page 33.)

• FINISHED MEASUREMENTS

16" x 20" (40 cm x 50 cm).

• MATERIALS

1/2 yd. (.5 m) orange checked cotton fabric 45" (115 cm) wide, 1/8 yd. (.1 m) orange cotton fabric, 45" (115 cm) wide, 7-1/4 yds (6.5 m) ecru polyester grosgrain ribbon 1-1/4"

(3 cm) wide, 2-1/4 yds (2 m) piping cord, 3/8" (1 cm) in diameter, zipper 12" (30 cm) long, thread, pillow form 16" x 20" (40 cm x 50 cm).

• **INSTRUCTIONS**

From the checked fabric cut one piece 21" x 17" (53 cm x 43 cm) for the front. Cut a piece 2-1/2" x 17" (6 cm x 43 cm) and a piece 19-1/2" x 17" (40 cm x 43 cm) for the back. From the orange fabric cut strips 2" (5 cm) wide, piecing them to make a single strip 78" (195 cm) long for the piping. Sew all pieces with right sides together and with 1/2" (1.5 cm) seam allowance.

Pin the 2 back pieces together along a 17" (43 cm) side. Stitch 2" (5 cm) in from each end with short stitches and baste the remainder of the seam. Press seam open. Center the zipper, wrong side up, over the wrong side of the basted seam and stitch in place. Remove the basting.

Cut the ribbon into 8 pieces 32" (81 cm) long. Pin 4 strips diagonally across the pillow back, taking care not to place ribbon over the zipper opening. Weave the ribbons as shown in the sketch, allowing the ends to extend beyond the edges of the fabric.

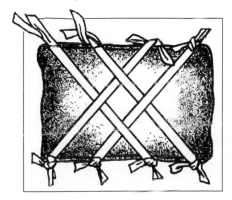

Crisscrossed Pillows

Stitch the ribbons in place along both edges, beginning and ending the stitching 2" (5 cm) from the edge of the fabric. Pin the ends of the ribbons toward the center of the fabric to keep them out of the way while the pillow is assembled. Repeat for the front of the pillow, arranging the ribbons in exactly the same pattern as is on the back so that the ends will meet at the edges.

Fold the piping strip tightly around the cord, right side out. With raw edges together, stitch as closely as possible to the cord, using a piping foot or zipper foot. Trim the seam allowance to 1/2" (1.5 cm). Place the pillow front right side up and pin the piping around the edges, beginning and ending at a corner and keeping raw edges together. Clip the piping seam allowance to the seamline at corners, and round the corners to match the pillow form. Stitch along the previous seamline, sewing the ends of the piping into the seams.

Pin the cushion back to the cushion front with right sides together. Stitch around all edges along the previous stitching line. Trim the corners and turn right side out. Insert the pillow form. Knot the ribbon ends together and trim the ends evenly, on the diagonal. ∎

FRINGED NAPKINS

℘

• **FINISHED MEASUREMENTS**

20" (51 cm) square.

• **MATERIALS**

For each napkin, orange checked cotton fabric 20" (51 cm) square, matching thread.

• **INSTRUCTIONS**

Cut each side of the napkin precisely by pulling a thread and cutting along it. To fringe all 4 edges, pull off the outer threads, one at a time, to a depth of 1" (2 cm). For a decorative finish and to prevent further raveling, wrap the fringe threads together in 1/4" (1 cm) bundles, catching the solid edge of the fabric between each bundle as shown in the sketches. ∎

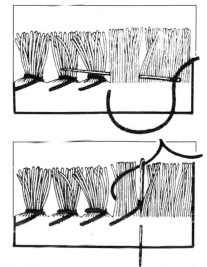

Finish the edges by wrapping the fringe threads in bundles.

ROOM IN SOFT ENGLISH PRINTS

.... ∽ ....

The large, graceful windows in this room bring in the blues and greens of sky and foliage. The fabric echoes those colors and adds pink and yellow floral accents. As an easy makeover for your favorite chair, there's a tied slipcover (page 40). A more tailored approach to seating is also included: patterns for covered cushions for the couch (page 41). Decorative accents consist of a fabric-covered vase (page 41), a folding screen with fabric panels (page 43), a braided wreath (page 44), and a ribbon picture hanger (page 45).

TIED CHAIR COVER

~

• MATERIALS

A king-size printed sheet, 108" x 108" (270 cm x 270 cm), or cotton print fabric pieced to desired size. Thread, cord.

• INSTRUCTIONS

Drape the fabric over chair to determine fit, tucking in around cushions. Allow extra fabric for draping and for hems. Stitch a 1/2" (1.5 cm) double hem around the edges.

For variations, tie knots

—at the front corners

—at the back corners or at center back

—at the end of each arm.

Allow extra fabric for knots, and tie knots before hemming. For another variation, gather up fabric to shape "flowers," tying them in place with cord as shown in the drawings. ■

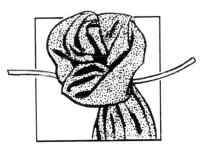

Vary the look of the tied chair
cover by making fabric "roses"
of the knotted material.

FABRIC-COVERED
VASE

ဆ

• **MATERIALS**

A vase, cotton print fabric, ribbon,
rubber band.

• **INSTRUCTIONS**

Place the fabric on a table, wrong
side up. Place a rubber band around
the neck of the vase. Set the vase at
the center of the fabric and fold the
fabric up around it. Tuck the ends of
the fabric under the rubber band.
Tie a ribbon around the neck of the
vase. ■

COVERED CUSHIONS

ဆ

(See photo on page 38.)

• **MATERIALS**

For each cushion: pillow form,
printed or striped cotton fabric,
thread, 1-1/4" yds (1.2 m) ribbon 1/4"
(1 cm) wide.

• **INSTRUCTIONS**

Measure the length and width of the
pillow form. Add 1/2" (1.5 cm) to all
edges and cut front from fabric. For
back, cut the same, but add 1-1/2" (4

cm) instead of 1/2" (1.5 cm) to one
edge (a narrow end for a rectangular
pillow form). Cut the back piece in
half widthwise. With right sides
together, stitch a 3/4" (2 cm) seam
across center back, leaving an
opening large enough to insert
pillow form. Stitch 3/4" (2 cm)
double hems in the seam allowances
of the opening. Cut the ribbon into 4
pieces. Sew the ends to the inner
edge of the opening, opposite each
other in pairs. Sew front to back
with right sides together and with
1/2" (1.5 cm) seam allowance. Trim
corners and turn right side out.
Insert pillow form. ■

Folding Screen with Fabric Panels

❧

• **Materials**

Three-panel folding screen with open upper panels, cotton print fabric for screen inserts, fabric printed with large bows, fusible interfacing, wallpaper paste, primer, white and colored enamel, paste and paint brushes. If screen does not have upper and lower rods in open sections, purchase 3 narrow spring tension rods to fit.

• **Instructions**

If screen is unpainted, paint first with primer. If previously painted, primer is unnecessary, but sand lightly before painting with enamel. When primer is thoroughly dry, sand lightly. Paint the frame of the screen with the desired color and paint the lower panels white.

Fuse interfacing to the wrong side of the bow motifs. Cut out motifs and spread wallpaper paste on the wrong sides. Glue motifs across centers of painted panels.

Curtains

Measure the open panels, or measure between rods if screen has them. Add 3" (8 cm) to the length and triple the width. Cut 3 pieces of fabric to these measurements. Stitch 1" (3 cm) double hems at sides. Fold upper edges 1-1/2" (4 cm) to inside; press. Turn under raw edges 1/2" (1.5 cm) and stitch close to folds. To form casings for the rods, stitch across tops, 1/4" (1 cm) below upper edge.

For screen with 6 rods, finish lower edges of curtains in the same way, but make the first fold 2-1/2" (6 cm) instead of 1-1/2" (4 cm). If 3 purchased rods are used, finish lower edges with 1" (3 cm) double hems. Place rods through casings and position in screen. ◼

Folding Screen Before Fabric Panels Are Attached

BRAIDED FABRIC WREATH

❧

• **FINISHED MEASUREMENTS**
11" (28 cm) diameter.

• **MATERIALS**
Strips of fabric in 3 different cotton prints, each 4" x 36" (10 cm x 90 cm), printed fabric 2-1/2" x 4-3/4" (6 cm x 12 cm), thread, fiberfill, 1-1/4 yds (1.2 m) striped ribbon 2-3/4" (7 cm) wide or printed fabric 5-1/2" x 46" (14 cm x 115 cm).

• **INSTRUCTIONS**
Fold the 3 fabric strips in half lengthwise with right sides together. Stitch the long edges with 1/4" (1 cm) seam allowance. Turn right side out and stuff firmly with fiberfill, leaving 1-1/2" (4 cm) at each end unstuffed. Stitch the ends closed, turning in raw edges. Braid the strips and stitch all ends together to form a circle.

Fold the remaining strip lengthwise with right sides together. Stitch the ends and long edge, leaving an opening for turning. Turn right side out and stitch the opening. Wrap around the wreath to cover the braid ends. Tie a bow with the ribbon and stitch it to the wreath. If a fabric strip is used instead of ribbon, stitch it as for the small fabric strip. ■

BOW PICTURE HANGER

❧

• **FINISHED MEASUREMENTS**
8-3/4" x 10-3/4" (22 cm x 27 cm).

• **MATERIALS**
White cotton fabric 14" x 16" (35 cm x 40 cm), fabric printed with rose motif 5-1/2" x 7" (14 cm x 18 cm), matching frame, fusible interfacing, white mat to fit frame, cardboard to fit frame. Blue/white vertically striped fabric 24" x 40" (60 cm x 100 cm), thread, small picture hook, small trimming scissors.

• **INSTRUCTIONS**
Fuse interfacing to the wrong side of the rose fabric and cut carefully around the edges of the motif. Center the motif on the white cotton and stitch it in place, stitching very close to the edges of the motif. Applique the motif using a close zigzag stitch, covering the edges of the motif and the line of straight stitching. Insert the mat and picture in the frame, and back with the cardboard.

Fold the long striped piece in half lengthwise, with right sides together. Stitch the long edge, leaving an opening at the center, and stitch diagonally across the ends. Trim corners and turn right side out. Stitch across the opening. Stitch the long edges of the shorter striped piece in the same way, but leave ends open. Turn right side out and press so seam is at center back. Fold the long strip into a bow. Gather the shorter piece to 1" (3 cm) across the center and wrap it around the center of the bow. Stitch in place. Sew the hook to center back of the bow. Staple the frame to the long ends as shown in the photo. ■

ROOM WITH STRIPED & FLORAL FABRIC

.... ∾ ....

Used generously, harmonizing fabrics can create a feeling of luxurious abundance. The fabrics in this living room are carried through to the sleeping area. Projects abound: scalloped curtains with bow ties (page 48), a buttoned quilt (page 50), a stenciled tray cloth (page 51), a tea cozy to keep the teapot warm through a second cup (page 52), a handsome covered lamp with matching shade (page 55), and a stenciled mirror with a fabric hanger (page 55).

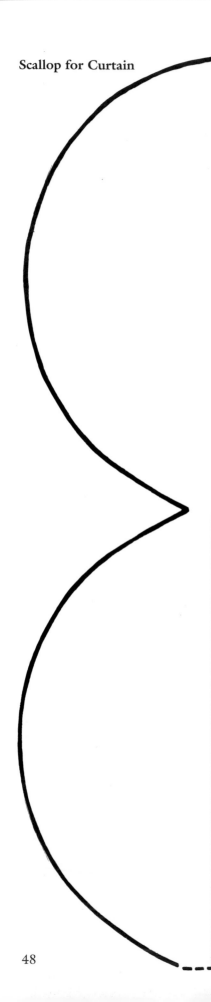

SCALLOPED CURTAINS WITH BOW TIES

• MATERIALS

Cotton fabric in 2 compatible floral prints, curtain rod, rings, light-weight cardboard. For the bow, 56" (1.4 m) of striped fabric 48" (120 cm) wide and flowered cotton 8-3/4" x 56" (22 cm x 140 cm), hook and loop tape.

• INSTRUCTIONS

Measure the width of the window. For each curtain, allow 1-1/2 to 2 times the width of half the window for pleats, plus 2-1/2" (6 cm) for side hems. Measure the length of the window. Subtract the width of the rings for the top of the curtain and add 8" (20 cm) for upper and lower hems. Cut flowered fabric according to these calculations.

Make a full-size template of the scallop motif on cardboard. From each cotton print cut 2 strips 3-1/4" (9 cm) wide and the length of the curtain minus the 8" (20 cm) hem allowance with 1/2" (1.5 cm) seam allowance added at each end. Beginning exactly 1/2" (1.5 cm) from the top of a strip, place the template on the wrong side of the fabric with the straight edge 1/2" (1.5 cm) from one edge of the fabric and the widest

point of the scallop 1/4" (1 cm) inside the other edge. Make the scalloped strips in pairs, one strip in each floral print with the scalloped edges facing each other, so that they will sew together correctly. Be sure the scallop pattern ends at the same point at the lower edge on both strips of a pair.

Place a pair of strips with right sides together. Stitch the scalloped edge along the pencil lines and stitch

across the ends with a 1/2" (1.5 cm) seam. Notch the curved edges almost to stitching line at 3/4" (2 cm) intervals. Turn right side out; press. Stitch long sides together with a zigzag stitch, overcasting the raw edges at the same time.

Stitch a 1-1/4" (3 cm) double hem on each side of each curtain. Pin the scalloped edge to the wrong side of the hemmed edge with 1/2" (1.5 cm)

overlap on the long edge and with the top and bottom of the scalloped strip 4" (10 cm) from the top and bottom of the curtain. Stitch in place. Press a 4" (10 cm) hem at the top and bottom of each curtain. Turn under raw edges 1/2" (1.5 cm), press, and stitch. Sew rings to the upper edges of the curtains, beginning and ending 1/4" (1 cm) from each side.

For each bow, cut a strip of striped fabric and a strip of flowered fabric 8-3/4" x 56" (22 cm x 140 cm). Stripes should run lengthwise. Cut a strip of the print fabric 8" x 28" (20 cm x 70 cm). Place the long strips with right sides together and stitch the long edges with 1/4" (1 cm) seam allowance, leaving an opening for turning. Sew diagonally across the narrow ends, beginning at a point 5-1/2" (14 cm) from the end on one long edge and tapering to 1/4" (1 cm) at the opposite corner. Trim corners and turn right side out.

Fold the shorter strip lengthwise with right sides together. Stitch ends and long edge with 1/4" (1 cm) seam allowance, leaving an opening on the long edge for turning. Trim corners and turn right side out. Attach hook and loop tape to the ends so that the ends can be fastened together in a ring. Fasten around the curtain at the desired height and tie the bow onto the ring. ■

Buttoned Quilt

∽

- **Finished Measurements**
74-3/4" x 90" (184 cm x 214 cm).

- **Materials**
28" x 60" (70 cm x 150 cm) cotton print fabric with ivy design, 1 yd (.9 m) x 52" (130 cm) cotton print fabric

with berry design, 48" (1.2 m) x 56" (140 cm) floral print cotton fabric. (*Note*: any 3 compatible cotton print fabrics could be substituted for the patterns given above.) 2-5/8 yds (2.2 m) lengthwise striped cotton fabric 48" (120 cm) wide, 80 buttons, acetate for quilting templates, thread, craft knife, rotary cutter and cutting mat or sharp scissors, ruler. For the batting and backing, fiberfill batting and cotton muslin 75-3/4" x 91" (187 cm x 217 cm).

• **INSTRUCTIONS**

The quilt consists of 5 rows of 4 patchwork blocks each, with 2-1/4" (5 cm) strips between them and with a 6" (15 cm) outer border. Each block is a square bordered with triangles to form a larger square.

Make a paper pattern 7" (17.5 cm) square. Cut it in half diagonally to form 2 triangles. Add 1/4" (1 cm) seam allowance to all sides of one of the triangles and cut an acetate stencil from the altered pattern. Cut a second stencil 10-3/4" (27 cm) square.

Using the templates, cut 40 triangles each from the ivy print and the berry print. From the floral print, cut 20 squares. Cut the following pieces on the lengthwise grain of the striped fabric: for outer lengthwise borders, 2 strips 6-3/4" x 79-1/2" (17 cm x 197 cm); for upper and lower crosswise borders, 2 strips 6-3/4" x 75-3/4" (17 cm x 187 cm); for crosswise strips between rows of blocks, 4 strips 2-3/4" x 63-1/4" (7 cm x 157 cm); for joining the blocks, 15 strips 2-3/4" x 14-1/2" (7 cm x 37 cm).

Sew all pieces with right sides together and with *exactly* 1/4" (1 cm) seam allowance. Press each seam open before sewing another seam across it.

To piece a block, sew the long sides of 2 ivy print triangles to opposite sides of a square. Sew 2 berry print

triangles to the other 2 sides of the square. Make 20 blocks this way.

Join 4 blocks with 3 of the short striped strips to form a crosswise row. Make a total of 5 rows. Join the rows with the 4 narrow striped strips. Sew the lengthwise borders to the sides of the quilt first, then sew the crosswise borders to the top and bottom.

Place the pieced front and the muslin backing with right sides together. Place the batting on top of the backing. Pin, and sew around the edges with 1/2" (1.5 cm) seam allowance, leaving an opening of 30" (70 cm) on one narrow end for turning. Trim the batting close to the stitching, and trim corners. Turn right side out and stitch across the opening. Sew a button at the center of each side of each square, sewing through all thicknesses. ■

STENCILED TRAY CLOTH

☙

• **FINISHED MEASUREMENTS**
26" x 45" (67 cm x 115 cm).

• **MATERIALS**
3/4 yd (.7 m) medium-weight linen in white or natural, 45" (115 cm) wide. Green and white textile paints, paper, carbon paper, stenciling acetate, craft knife, brush.

• **INSTRUCTIONS**
Make a full-size paper pattern of the motif and trace onto acetate. Cut out the motif. Mark lengthwise center of the cloth about 6" (15 cm) from each

end. Position the template with the end of the pattern at center and the bottom of the pattern about 5" (12.5 cm) from the end of the cloth. Outline the motif lightly in pencil. Repeat at the other side of center, matching the ends of the pattern. Then outline the pattern once more at each end. Repeat for the other end of the cloth.

Paint the designs, using a fairly dry brush. Mix the green and white paints to create intermediate shades as desired. Let the paint dry and heat-set according to the instructions with the paint.

To fringe the ends, pull off threads, one at a time, to a depth of about 1" (3 cm). Sew across the fabric at the end of the fringe to prevent further raveling. Stitch 1/2" (1.5 cm) double hems along the sides. ■

Stenciled Tray Cloth Motif

TEA COZY

&

• **FINISHED MEASUREMENTS**
13-1/4" x 18" (33 cm x 45 cm).

• **MATERIALS**
12" x 56" (30 cm x 140 cm) floral print cotton fabric, 8" (20 cm) cotton fabric in a coordinating print about 52" (130 cm) wide, 4" (10 cm) striped cotton fabric 48" (120 cm) wide, 16"

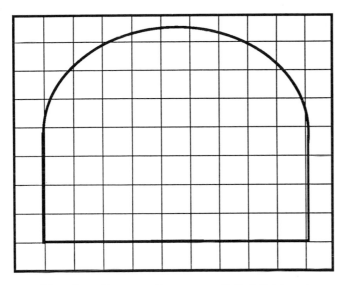

Tea Cozy Pattern. 1 square = 1-1/2" (4 cm).

(40 cm) white cotton fabric about 56" (140 cm) wide. Paper, light-weight cardboard, craft knife, heavy fusible interfacing, fiberfill batting.

• INSTRUCTIONS

For the tea cozy, make a full-size paper pattern from the graph, adding 1/4" (1 cm) seam allowance to all edges. Make a full-size pattern of the scallop motif with 9 scallops, adding 1/4" (1 cm) to the straight edge and ends, and outline it on the cardboard to make a template. Cut the template.

Double the primary floral print fabric and cut the body of the tea cozy. Double the white fabric and cut the body 2 times. Cut the body piece 2 times from the batting. For the trim, cut 2 strips of striped fabric 2-3/4" x 27" (7 cm x 68 cm). For the bow, cut 2 strips of striped fabric 1-1/4" x 10" (3 cm x 25 cm). From the second print, with the fabric doubled, cut 2 strips 3-3/4" x 30-1/4" (9.5 cm x 76 cm) for the scallops.

Using the template, outline the scallop pattern on the fusible interfacing and on the wrong side of one of the scallop strips. Trim seam allowances from the ends and straight edge of the interfacing. Fuse interfacing to the scallop strip. Pin

the 2 scallop strips with right sides together. Stitch the scalloped edge along the interfacing lines and stitch the ends with 1/2" (1 cm) seam allowance, leaving the long straight edge open. Notch the curved edges almost to the stitching, turn right side out, and press. Stitch the long edges together just inside the seamline.

Place the 2 printed tea cozy pieces with right sides together and the scalloped band between them, aligning all raw edges. Stitch, with 1/4" (1 cm) seam allowance, clipping the seam allowance of the scalloped band where necessary.

With right sides together and 1/4" (1 cm) seam allowance, stitch the 2 longer striped pieces together at the ends to form a ring. Press under 1/4" (1 cm) on one long edge. Sew the un-pressed edge around the lower edge of the tea cozy with right sides together with 1/4" (1 cm) seam allowance.

Stitch the lining sections together in pairs with right sides together, sewing only the curved edges and using 1/2" (1.5 cm) seam allowance. Clip the seams. Trim 1/2" (1.5 cm) from the curved edges of the batting pieces. Abut the edges and sew together with a zigzag stitch. Place the batting between the linings so

that both lining pieces are right side out. Align lower raw edges and stitch together with 1/4" (1 cm) seam allowance. Trim batting close to stitching. Put the padded lining inside the tea cozy, align the lower stitching lines, pin in place. Fold the pressed edge of the trim to the inside, just covering the stitching line on the lining. Pin, and stitch close to the fold through all thicknesses.

Sew the remaining striped strips with right sides together and 1/4" (1 cm) seam allowance. Stitch around all edges, leaving an opening on one long side for turning. Trim corners, turn right side out, and stitch across the opening. Tie a bow and stitch it to the front of the tea cozy. ■

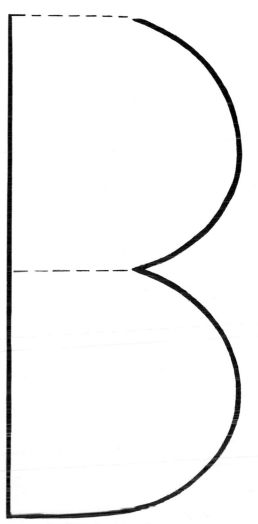

Scallop for Tea Cozy

COVERED LAMP AND SHADE

∽

• MATERIALS

LAMPSHADE

A lampshade form with a wide bottom opening, floral print cotton fabric, single fold bias tape 1/4" (1 cm) wide. Lamp base. Striped chintz fabric, thread, kraft paper.

• INSTRUCTIONS

BASE

Measure from the top of the base to center of the bottom. On kraft paper, make a circular pattern with this measurement plus 3/4" (2 cm) as the radius. Use the pattern to cut a circle from the striped fabric. Cut a strip of fabric 2" (5 cm) wide and the circumference of the base plus 1-1/4" (3 cm) in length. Place the circle wrong side up on a table. Place the lamp precisely in the center. Fold the fabric up around the base, forming pleats at least 1/4" (1 cm) wide. Hand stitch the pleats in place. Trim the upper edge evenly. Fold under 1/4" (1 cm) on the long edges of the strip; press. Wrap strip around the top to cover raw edges of the pleats. Turn under the overlapping end and stitch in place.

LAMPSHADE

Wrap bias tape solidly around upper and lower rings of the form. Stitch ends in place. Measure the height of the form. Cut a piece of fabric the width of this measurement plus 2-1/2" (6 cm) and as long as the circumference of the lower ring plus 1/2" (1.5 cm). Cut a strip of fabric

1-3/4" (4.5 cm) wide and as long as the circumference of the upper ring plus 3/4" (2 cm). With right sides together and with 1/4" (1 cm) seam allowance, stitch the ends of the lampshade fabric to form a ring. Press the seam open. Press the raw edges 1/4" (1 cm) to wrong side. Fold the lower edge of the fabric under the lower ring of the form and stitch in place. Fold the upper edge over the upper ring, pleating evenly around, and stitch in place. Press under 1/4" (1 cm) on the long edges of the strip, and press it in half lengthwise, right side out. Fold the strip over the top of the shade and stitch it in place, turning under the overlapping end. ■

STENCILED MIRROR WITH BOWS

∽

• MATERIALS

A mirror with a wooden frame, green and white hobby paint, carbon paper, stenciling acetate, craft knife, stenciling brush. For the bow, 32" (.8 m) floral print cotton fabric 56" (140 cm) wide, thread, small curtain ring, small tacks, picture hook.

• INSTRUCTIONS

Make a full-size drawing of the motif and trace onto the acetate. Cut out the motif with a craft knife. Mix a small amount of the green and white paints to obtain a light green shade. Place the acetate at top center of the mirror frame. Paint the motif. Remove excess paint from the brush onto scrap paper and hold the brush

vertically so paint won't run under acetate. Paint the flower and the dot light green, and the leaves and the arch green. Paint 3 motifs to each side of center. Paint one motif with 4 extra leaves at the center of each side, and 5 motifs at the bottom of the mirror. Paint light green dots between the groups of motifs, and a green line around the inside of the frame.

For the bow, cut 4 strips of fabric 7-1/2" x 56" (19 cm x 140 cm). Sew all seams with right sides together and with 1/2" (1.5 cm) seam allowance.

Stenciled Motif Pattern

Sew 2 strips together at one end to make one long strip. Repeat with the other pair. Fold the strips in half lengthwise and sew long edges together, leaving an opening for turning. Sew diagonally across the ends, beginning at a point 6-3/4" (17 cm) from the end on one side and tapering to the seamline at the opposite corner. Trim corners and turn right side out. Tie a bow, leaving the ends about 12" (30 cm) long.

Attach the bow ends to the wrong side of the mirror with small tacks so that the bow shows above the mirror as in the photo. Sew a ring to the back of the bow knot to hang the mirror. ■

Loose Cover
for an
Overstuffed
Chair

⌇

• MATERIALS

Pink or yellow cotton chintz, non-woven pattern drafting material or muslin, felt-tip pen.

• INSTRUCTIONS

Pin pattern-drafting material or muslin to the chair to make pattern pieces. Make a pattern of the back of the chair from center top to floor, the inner back from center top to seat, outer arms from center top to floor, inner arms from center top to seat, seat from the back down the front to the floor, and the fronts of the arms. Allow ease for tucks on rounded edges and allow about 5" (13 cm) ease on sides and back of seat, inner arms, and inner back to tuck in around the cushion.

Pin pattern pieces together on the chair and mark the seamlines. Cut the pieces from chintz, adding 1/2" (1.5 cm) seam allowances and 2" (5 cm) for hem. Sew the pieces with right sides together. Sew inner and outer back pieces together. Sew inner and outer arm pieces together, and sew to back. Sew seat to back and to inner arms. Sew front arm pieces in place. Stitch a 2" (5 cm) double hem around the lower edge. ■

FITTED CHAIR COVER

• MATERIALS

For the chair shown in the photo:
4 yds (3.5 m) fabric 60" (150 cm)
wide, gridded pattern-drafting
material or muslin, stiff plastic,
2-1/2 yds (2.2 m) piping cord,
zipper 26" (65 cm) long.

• INSTRUCTIONS

Make a full-size paper pattern from
the graph. Cut the pieces from
pattern-drafting material or muslin,
adding 1/2" (1.5 cm) seam allowance.
Cut 2 each of the inner and outer
arms and the gussets, turning the
pattern piece upside down to cut the

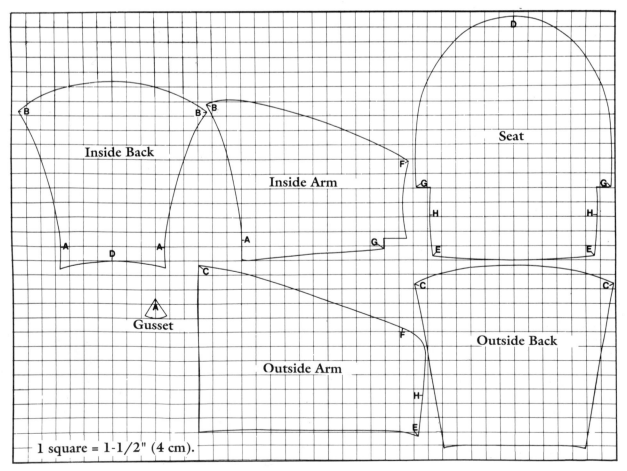

Inside Back

Inside Arm

Seat

Gusset

Outside Arm

Outside Back

1 square = 1-1/2" (4 cm).

seam on one side for the zipper.

Sew the outer piece to the inner piece and seat. To reinforce this seam and the seam around the seat, sew a second line of stitching 1/8" (.5 cm) inside the first. Trim the seams.

To make the piping, fold the ends of the strip 1/4" (1 cm) to the wrong side. Fold the strip in half, right side out, around the cord. Sew the edges together, stitching as closely as possible to the cord. Pin the piping around the lower edge of the cover, on the right side, with raw edges together. Begin and end the piping at the zipper seam. Stitch piping to the cover along the piping stitching line. Sew the ends closed.

Fold the skirt pieces in half, with right sides together, to a width of 10-3/4" (27 cm). Sew the side seams with 1/4" (1 cm) seam allowance.

second one. Cut a piece 21-1/2" x 24" (54 cm x 60 cm) for the front skirt, 2 pieces 21-1/2" x 22-3/4" (54 cm x 57 cm) for the side skirts, and 1 piece 21-1/2" x 16-3/4" (54 cm x 42 cm) for the back skirt. For pleat underlays, cut 3 pieces 8-3/4" x 11" (22 cm x 28 cm) and 2 pieces 5" x 11" (12.5 cm x 28 cm). For the piping, cut bias strips 1-1/4" (1.5 cm) wide and piece them as necessary to a length of 84-3/4" (212 cm). Cut one piece of plastic 10-1/4" x 23-1/2" (26 cm x 59 cm) and 2 pieces 10-1/4" x 16-1/4" (26 cm x 41 cm).

Pin the pieces together on the chair and adjust the fit. Cut the altered pattern pieces from fabric. Sew all pieces with right sides together and with 1/2" (1.5 cm) seam allowance.

Sew the inner back to the inner arm pieces, inserting the gussets at the lower edge. Sew the seat in place. Sew the outer arms to the outer back, basting the lower end of the

Trim the seams and turn right side out. Insert the plastic pieces. With right sides together, sew the skirt pieces to the cover, using 1/2" (1.5 cm) seam allowance on the top and 1/4" (1 cm) on the skirt.

Stitch a 1/4" (1 cm) single hem at the lower edge of each of the 3 pleat underlay pieces. Sew the pieces at the side front seams and at the back seam without the zipper. Stitch a 1/4" (1 cm) single hem along one long edge and the lower edge of the 2 small underlay pieces. Press the other long edge of each piece 1/2" (1.5 cm) to the wrong side. Place these pieces at the zipper seam. Pin the tops of these pieces even with the seam of the skirt pieces and stitch in place. Baste the 2 small pieces together at the pressed edges, abutting the edges and using a long zigzag stitch. Insert the zipper in the basted seam. ■

STRIPED SLIPCOVER

∾

• **MATERIALS**
Striped fabric, non-woven pattern-drafting material or muslin, thread, tape measure, felt-tip pen, pins. Zipper, if needed.

• **INSTRUCTIONS**
Using pattern-drafting material or muslin, make a full-size pattern of the back of the chair to the floor, a pattern of the inner chair back from top to seat, a pattern of the outer

and inner arms, beginning at the seat and measuring over the arm to the floor, and a pattern of the seat from back to front and down the front to the floor. If the chair has a loose seat cushion, the cushion can be covered separately, in which case the chair should be measured without the cushion, or the entire chair and cushion can be covered as one piece. Pin the pattern-drafting material on the chair to make the pattern pieces, fitting carefully. Don't fit the cover too tightly, and allow a generous amount of ease where the inner back and inner arms join the seat. Mark all seamlines with felt-tip pen.

Make a second set of pattern pieces, adding 1/2" (1.5 cm) seam allowance on all edges and 2" (5 cm) for hems. Cut the arm pattern from doubled fabric to ensure a right and a left side. Cut all other pieces singly. Center a stripe at the center back and center front of the chair. On the other pieces, match stripes wherever possible.

Sew the pieces with right sides together. If the chair is wider at the top than at the bottom, insert a zipper at a side back seam. Sew the back and arm pieces together first, then sew the front and seat sections to the inner edges of the arm pieces. Stitch a 2" (5 cm) double hem around the bottom. ■

HUNGARIAN APPLIQUE

············ ❦ ············

Black and white provide the sharpest color contrast. Add images with crisp, clear lines, and you get striking furnishings for the living room.

The technique known as Hungarian applique involves basting a paper pattern onto two pieces of fabric—in this case, white felt over black cotton—stitching along the lines of the motif, then cutting away all of the white felt that's not part of the design. The technique lends itself to a variety of projects, including pillows, covers for director's chairs (both shown on this page), and a handsome throw (shown on page 71).

HUNGARIAN APPLIQUE
STEP BY STEP

Tip

Use an even-feed presser foot or reduce presser foot pressure to prevent distorting the felt applique when stitching.

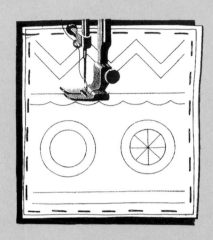

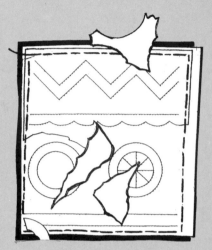

1. Make a full-size paper pattern. Trace the pattern on tear-away backing, using a felt-tip fabric marker with wash-out or disappearing ink. Make a separate tracing for each applique. Pin the tracing to the white felt, position the felt on the black fabric, and baste through all 3 layers. Machine stitch along the design lines of the pattern.

2. Remove the tear-away backing very carefully after stitching, using tweezers in the small design areas.

3. With applique scissors or small sharp scissors, cut away the small design areas inside the motif. Take care to cut only through the felt.

4. Cut away large sections of the motif, leaving narrow margins outside the stitching lines.

5. For the paisley motif, cut around the outer edges of the motif with pinking shears, leaving at least 1/8" (.5 cm) outside the stitching line.

BLACK AND WHITE APPLIQUED PILLOWS

ৎ

(See photo on page 62.)

• FINISHED MEASUREMENTS

16" (40 cm) square.

• MATERIALS

For each pillow, 2 pieces black cotton fabric 17" (46 cm) square, extra fabric for fringe, white felt, tear-away backing, felt-tip fabric marker with wash-out or disappearing ink, white and black thread, applique or sharp trimming scissors, pinking shears, tweezers, pillow form.

• INSTRUCTIONS

Using the photograph as a guide, prepare full-size paper patterns of desired motifs. Trace the patterns and baste to felt according to the step-by-step instructions. Baste the designs to cotton squares, keeping the design within 1" (3 cm) of the edges of the square. Stitch and trim the designs.

For fringe, cut a strip of cotton fabric 2-3/4" (7 cm) wide and 15" long on the cross grain of the fabric, allowing one strip for each fringed edge desired. Along one long edge of the strip make cuts at 1/8" (.5 cm) intervals to within 1/2" (1.5 cm) of the other long edge. Baste each strip to the right side of the pillow front, matching solid long edge of the strip to raw edge of the pillow front and with ends of the strip 1/2" (1.5 cm) from edges of the pillow front.

Stitch pillow front to pillow back with 1/2" (1.5 cm) seams, taking care not to catch fringe in seam. Leave an opening along one edge large enough to insert pillow form. Clip corners and turn right side out. Insert pillow form and slipstitch opening. ■

Paisley Pattern for Appliqued Pillow

Patterns for Appliqued Pillows.
Shown 90% of actual size; photocopy at 111%.

Appliqued Director's Chair Cover

⌇

(See photo on page 62.)

• Materials

Black cotton fabric, white felt, applique scissors or sharp trimming scissors, tweezers, tear-away backing, fabric marking pen with wash-out or disappearing ink, white and black thread.

• Instructions

Measure the chair for the cover. Measure outer back from top of chair to floor, inner back from top of chair to seat, outer side from top center of arm to floor, inner side from top center of arm to seat, seat from back to front and side to side, and front from side to side and from seat to floor. Make a paper pattern for each piece, adding 1/2" (1.5 cm) seam allowance to each edge and adding ease and hem allowance as instructed for each piece. Outer back: add 1" (3 cm) at lower edge for hem and 1" (3 cm) at top and at each side for ease; cut 1 from fabric. Inner back: cut 1. Outer side: add 1" (3 cm) at lower edge for hem and 1" (3 cm) ease at each side; cut 2. Inner side: cut 2. Seat: cut 1. Front: add 1" (3 cm) ease at lower edge.

Work applique on the outer back and 2 outer sides. Place the design 3" (8 cm) from the top of the piece and center it between the sides. Follow the step-by-step instructions for the applique.

Assemble the chair cover, sewing all pieces with right sides together and

Pattern for Director's Chair Cover. Shown 90% of actual size; photocopy at 111%.

making tucks at corners where necessary for fit. Sew outer sides to outer back, matching lower edges. Sew inner sides to outer sides across arms. Sew inner back to outer back above arms and across top. Sew inner back to inner sides below arms. Sew the front to the seat. Sew seat to inner sides and to inner back. Sew outer sides to inner sides and front, leaving open the lower 12" (30 cm). Make a double hem in the seam allowances along the open edges. Make a 1" (3 cm) double hem around the lower edge of the cover. ■

APPLIQUED THROW

(See photo on page 71.)

• **FINISHED MEASUREMENTS**

65" x 80" (162 cm x 199 cm).

• **MATERIALS**

2-1/4 yds (2.1 m) black felt 72" (180 cm) wide, 1-1/4 yds (1 m) white felt 72" (180 cm) wide, 4 yds (3.7 m) tear-away backing, white and black

thread, kraft paper, small trimming scissors, pinking shears, fabric marker with water-soluble or disappearing ink, waterproof marking pen.

• **INSTRUCTIONS**

Cut a 7" (18 cm) strip from one long edge of the black felt. Make full-size paper patterns of the motifs, using a permanent marker. Trace 4 corner motifs and 6 straight motifs onto tear-away backing with a fabric marking pen. Trace 2 of the corner

motifs with the pattern right side up and 2 with it upside down.

For the upper edge of the design, place 2 of the corner sections together so that the long edges meet. Overlap the circle and paisley at the ends of the 2 pieces to form a continuous design for the top and corners. Pin the piece to the white felt, allowing 3/4" (2 cm) around the outer and inner edges of the design. Cut away one layer of the traced backing where the pieces overlap. Make another piece this way for the lower edge and corners.

For each side, place 3 of the straight motif sections together, overlapping the ends as for the top and bottom. Pin these to white felt and cut them, leaving 3/4" (2 cm) beyond the design lines at the outer and inner edges.

Center the pieces on the black felt, overlapping the side pieces and the corner pieces where they meet, as before. Cut away one layer of backing where the pieces overlap. Carefully cut away one layer of the felt at this point too, so that the ends of the felt meet evenly, but do not overlap. Pin the design in place.

Stitch along all design lines, following the step-by-step instructions and using the photo as a guide. With pinking shears, trim away the white felt around the outer border of the design, cutting 1/2" (1.5 cm) outside the stitching line.

Stitch around the outer edge of the throw, 2-1/2" (6.5 cm) from the edge. To make the fringe, cut from the edge to the stitching line at 1/4" (1 cm) intervals all around the throw. ■

Pattern for Appliqued Throw. Shown at 55% of actual size; photocopy at 182%.

YELLOW
COUNTRY
KITCHEN

.... ✌ ....

Some cooks say that yellow is the very best color for a kitchen: sunny and warm, cheerful and welcoming. Certainly it's popular for country kitchens and dining rooms, whether in small accents or larger projects. Both types of projects appear on the following pages. There are ruffled shelf borders and stenciled potholders (page 74), a fabric cover for a recipe holder (page 76), curtains and a crisscrossed tablecloth (page 77), a chair cushion and an oven mitt (pages 78 and 79), fringed jar tops and three decorated baskets (page 80).

RUFFLED SHELF BORDERS

∽

• **MATERIALS**

Lightweight fabric in two complementary prints, thread.

• **INSTRUCTIONS**

Measure the length of the shelf. From one print fabric cut a strip this length plus 1" (3 cm) and 3-1/2" (9 cm) wide. For the ruffle cut a strip from the other print 2-1/2 times the length of the shelf and 4" (10 cm) wide.

Hem the ends and one long edge of each strip with a 1/2" (1.5 cm) double hem. Using a long machine stitch, sew 2 rows along the raw edge of the ruffle, 3/8" and 5/8" (1 cm and 2 cm) from the edge. Draw up the bobbin threads to gather the ruffle to the length of the shorter strip. Sew the 2 pieces, with right sides together and with 1/2" (1.5 cm) seam allowance. Tack the strip over the edge of the shelf. ■

STENCILED POTHOLDER

∽

• **FINISHED MEASUREMENTS**

8" x 8" (20 x 20 cm).

• **MATERIALS**

Use 100% cotton fabric. Print fabric 20" x 20" (51 cm x 51 cm), fiberfill batting 10" x 10" (25 cm x 25 cm),

tracing paper, acetate, craft knife, stenciling brush, fabric paint, thread.

• **INSTRUCTIONS**

Cut 2 pieces of cotton 10" (25 cm) square. Cut 1-1/2" (4 cm) strips, stitching the ends together to make a continuous strip 38" (96 cm) long. With right sides together, stitch the ends of the long strip together to form a loop for the trim.

Trace the motif, then trace it onto acetate. Cut the motif out of the acetate. Position the stencil at one corner of a fabric square, 2" (5 cm) from each edge. Mix the paint in a small dish, dip the brush, and remove excess paint on scrap paper. Paint the stencil, holding brush vertically so paint doesn't run under edges of the acetate. Repeat for the second fabric square. Allow paint to dry, and heat set according to

manufacturer's directions.

Sandwich the fabric squares with wrong sides together and the batting between them, with the motif in the same corner top and bottom. Machine quilt through all thicknesses, stitching diagonal rows 1-1/4" (3 cm) apart, first in one direction then in the other to form a diamond pattern. Round the corners. Stitch around the potholder 1/4" (1 cm) from the edge.

Starting at a corner, stitch trim around the edges of the potholder with right sides together. Keep raw edges even and use 1/2" (1 cm) seam allowance. The excess trim will form a loop at the beginning corner. Fold the trim over the raw edge of the potholder and fold in the raw edge of the trim. Press. Stitch the trim around the potholder close to the fold, and continue stitching around the doubled edges of the loop. ■

**Pattern for Stencil.
Use a stubby stenciling
brush and very little paint.**

RECIPE FOLDER

~

• **FINISHED MEASUREMENTS**
10-1/2" x 13-1/4" (26.5 cm x 33 cm).

• **MATERIALS**
Two pieces of heavy cardboard
10-1/2" x 13-1/4" (26.5 cm x 33 cm).
Two pieces of brown kraft paper
10-1/4" x 16" (26 cm x 40 cm).
Yellow print fabric, a piece 16" x 24"
(40 cm x 60 cm), 2 strips 3-1/4" x 12"
(8 cm x 30 cm), and a strip 1" x
12-3/4" (3 cm x 31 cm). A strip of
fusible interfacing 3/4" x 13-1/4"
(2 cm x 33 cm). Two pieces of heavy
white paper 10-1/4" x 12-3/4" (25.5
cm x 31 cm). A piece of white cotton
3-1/2" x 4-3/4" (9 cm x 12 cm). White
glue, paste brush, craft knife,
waterproof felt-tip marker.

• **INSTRUCTIONS**
Place the large piece of fabric wrong
side up. Position the 2 pieces of
cardboard on the fabric 1" (2.5 cm)
from the edges and with 3/4" (2 cm)
between them for the spine of the
book. Outline the cardboard pieces
with pencil. Fuse interfacing strip to
the wrong side of the fabric at the
spine. Cut diagonally across the
4 outer corners of the fabric 1/4"
(1 cm) outside the corners of the
cardboard outline. Spread glue on
one side and around all edges of the
cardboard pieces. Glue to the wrong
side of the fabric within the outline.
Fold the edges of the fabric to the
inside, corners first, and glue in place.

On the pieces of kraft paper mark a point 3-1/4" (8 cm) in from the right edge at the top and at the bottom. Mark a point the same distance up from the bottom and down from the top on the right edge. Draw a line connecting the 2 points at the upper corner, and another line connecting the 2 points at the lower corner. Cut off the corner triangles. Position the pieces of paper on the front and back of the book, centered vertically and with the long edges 1-1/2" (4 cm) from the spine. Glue in place. Fold the outer edges of the paper to the inside of the covers and glue.

Fold the 2 cotton strips in half lengthwise, right sides together. Stitch long edges and across 1 end. Turn right side out. Glue 2" (5 cm) of the unfinished end of each tie inside each cover at the midpoint of the outer edge, so that the ties lie perpendicular to the edges of the cover with the finished ends outward.

Position the pieces of white paper inside the covers 1/4" (1 cm) from the outer edges. Glue in place. Glue the remaining fabric strip over the spine on the inside of the book.

Write the title on the small piece of white cotton with waterproof marker. Glue it to the front cover. ■

CRISSCROSSED TABLECLOTH

(See photo on page 72.)

• **FINISHED MEASUREMENTS**
40" x 40" (100 cm x 100 cm).

• **MATERIALS**
Yellow fabric in a small floral print, blue floral print fabric, yellow fabric with a large floral print, thread.

• **INSTRUCTIONS**
From the yellow small floral print, cut a piece 42-1/2" (106 cm) square. From the blue print, cut 4 strips 2-1/2" x 42-1/2" (6 cm x 106 cm). From the yellow large floral, cut 4 pieces 7-3/4" (19.5 cm) square.

Position the small squares on the corners of the tablecloth with all

pieces right side up, aligning the outer edges. Baste in place. Fold under the long edges of the blue strips 1/2" (1.5 cm) and press. Position a strip parallel to one edge of the tablecloth, 7-1/4" (18.5 cm) from the edge, so it overlaps the inner edge of the 2 small squares by 1/2" (1.5 cm). Stitch in place along folded edges of the strip. Repeat with the other 3 strips.

Fold a 1-1/4" (3 cm) hem around the outer edges of the cloth; press. Turn under the raw edge 1/4" (1 cm) and stitch. ■

CURTAINS

• **FINISHED MEASUREMENTS**
Two curtains, each 35" (90 cm) across top, 20" (54 cm) long, excluding ties.

• **MATERIALS**
Yellow print cotton 54" (140 cm) wide, 1-1/2 yds (1.4 m). Blue print cotton 36" (90 cm) wide, 1/2 yd. (.4 m). Thread, curtain rod.

• **INSTRUCTIONS**
For curtains, cut 2 pieces of yellow fabric each 22-1/2" (60 cm) long and the width of the fabric. Fold side edges to inside 1-1/4" (3 cm) and press. Turn under raw edges 1/4" (1 cm), press and stitch. Hem bottom and top edges in the same way. At top of curtain make 11 pleats, each 3/4" (2 cm) deep. Make the first pleats at the side hems and space the others evenly—about 3-1/2" (9 cm) apart across the curtain. Press the pleats and stitch them along hem stitching line and close to top edge.

For tie carriers, cut 2 strips 1-1/2" x 27-1/2" (4 cm x 71.5 cm) from yellow print fabric. Fold strips in half lengthwise, right sides together, and stitch long edges with 1/4" (1 cm) seam allowance. Turn right side out. Cut each strip into 11 pieces, each 2-1/2" (6.5 cm) long. Fold each short strip to make a loop, as shown in the drawing. Place one over each pleat on wrong side of curtain. Align ends at hemline and stitch ends to curtain along the hem stitching line.

For ties, stitch a 1/4" (1 cm) hem at top and bottom edges of blue print fabric. Cut the piece, lengthwise, into 22 strips 1-1/2" (4 cm) wide. Fold strips in half lengthwise, right sides together, and stitch long edges with 1/4" (1 cm) seam allowance. Turn right side out. Pull each tie through a carrier on the curtain, and tie over the rod. ■

Ruffled
Chair Cushion

• **MATERIALS**

Cotton print fabric, fiberfill batting, thread.

• **INSTRUCTIONS**

Make a paper pattern of the seat, cutting out a little at back corners and rounding front corners. Cut 1 piece from batting. Add 1/4" (1 cm) seam allowance around all edges, and cut 2 pieces from fabric.

Determine length of the 2 ruffles: measure sides and front of seat for one, and measure between back corners for the other. Cut a strip twice the length of each of these measurements and 7" (18 cm) wide. Hem ends of the strips with 1/2" (1.5 cm) double hems. Fold the strips in half lengthwise, right side out, and sew raw edges together with 2 rows

of machine basting stitch, 3/8" and 5/8" (1 cm and 2 cm) from the edge. Draw up bobbin threads to gather ruffles to fit cushion, and pin to one cushion piece.

For the ties, cut 4 strips 1-1/2" x 16-3/4" (4 cm x 42 cm). Fold lengthwise, right sides together, and stitch long edges with a narrow seam allowance. Turn right side out.

Place the 2 cushion pieces right sides together. Place batting on top and pin 2 ties at each back corner. Stitch around edges, leaving an opening for turning. Turn right side out and stitch across the opening. ■

Oven Mitt

• **Finished Measurements**
6-1/4" x 24" (16 cm x 60 cm).

• MATERIALS

Use only 100% cotton fabric. Yellow fabric with large floral print, 14" x 25" (36 cm x 64 cm). Blue floral print fabric, 21" x 42" (53 cm x 107 cm). Yellow fabric with small floral print, 2 strips, each 1-1/4" x 6-1/4" (3 cm x 16 cm). Fiberfill batting 13" x 25" (53 cm x 107 cm), thread, tracing paper.

• INSTRUCTIONS

Fold tracing paper in half, align fold with straight end of pattern, and trace pattern so that unfolded tracing is rounded at both ends.

From the blue print fabric, cut 2 pieces with the traced pattern folded in half. Cut 1 piece 14" x 25" (36 cm x 64 cm). From the remaining piece, cut bias strips 1-1/2" (4 cm) wide. Sew ends of the strips together to make a bias strip 55" (140 cm) long.

Cut the batting in half, lengthwise. Fold the large piece of yellow fabric in half lengthwise, right side out, and place a piece of batting between the layers. Machine quilt through all thicknesses. Stitch on the diagonal, keeping stitching lines about 1-1/2" (4 cm) apart. Then stitch on the diagonal in the other direction to create a diamond pattern. Quilt the large piece of blue fabric in the same way. With the pattern unfolded, cut one from each quilted piece.

Cut 4" (10 cm) from the straight ends of the 2 unquilted blue pieces. Position one of the yellow print strips across the cut end of each piece, with *right* side of yellow strip to the *wrong* side of the blue. Align raw edges and stitch, using 1/4" (1 cm) seam allowance. Turn strip to right side, fold raw edge under, press, and stitch again close to edge of trim.

Position the yellow quilted piece on the blue quilted piece, and place the blue unquilted ends on top, right sides up. Stitch around the outer edge through all layers with 1/4" (1 cm) seam allowance.

Fold the long bias strip in half lengthwise, right side out. Press. Fold both raw edges in to center and press. Fold the strip over the outer edge of the mitt. Stitch close to the inner edge of the trim through all layers, turning under the raw edge at the end. ■

FRINGED JAR TOPS

(See photo on page 75.)

• MATERIALS

Jars with lids, cotton print fabric, twine, lightweight cardboard.

• INSTRUCTIONS

Measure the diameter of the jar lids. Cut fabric squares 2" (5 cm) wider than the lid diameter. Pull threads to fringe the outer 1/8" (.5 cm) of each edge. Cut cardboard labels and sew one in the center of each fabric square with a zigzag stitch. Tie the fabric over the lids with twine. ■

THREE DECORATED BASKETS

(Also see photo on page 79.)

• MATERIALS

Baskets with handles, cotton print fabric, thin fiberfill batting, thread, white glue.

FLAT BASKET WITH HANDLE

Cut a fabric strip 4-3/4" x 48" (12 cm x 122 cm) to cover the handle and another piece 8" x 48" (20 cm x 120 cm) for the bow. Fold the first strip in half lengthwise, right sides together, and stitch the long edge. Turn right side out. Sew one end of the strip to the base of the handle on one side. Wrap around handle, and sew the other end in place. Fold the second fabric strip in half lengthwise, right sides together. Stitch the ends on the diagonal, and stitch the long edge, leaving an opening at the center for turning. Turn right side out and stitch the opening. Tie the bow around the handle as illustrated.

TALL BASKET WITH SMALL HANDLES

Cut a fabric strip 4" (10 cm) wide. Hem the long edges with a 1/4" (1 cm) single hem. Insert one end of the strip above the lower edge of the basket from inside to outside and return to inside under upper rim of basket. Continue around the basket, and tie the ends. Adjust fabric so the strip is right side out all around the basket.

FLAT BASKET WITH SMALL HANDLES

Measure the diameter of the basket top. Cut a fabric circle the diameter of the basket plus twice the height plus 4-3/4" (12 cm). Cut a circle the same size from fiberfill batting. Position the batting on the wrong side of the fabric circle and center the basket on the batting. Fold up the fabric around the sides of the basket, forming pleats. Remove the basket and stitch a 1-1/4" (3 cm) single hem around the top of the fabric through all layers. Replace the basket in the fabric cover. Fold the fabric over the top of the basket and glue in place, clipping to fit around handles. ■

POTPOURRI

.... 𝔰 ....

Fragrance adds a new dimension to a room's attractiveness. Dried herbs and flowers, known as potpourri, have graced homes across countless centuries and cultures.

Potpourri can be good-looking as well as sweet-smelling if it's encased in attractive fabric. For your country home, make a few pocket potpourris, cover an herb-filled jar with an attractive top, shape some potpourris like hearts or cats, or attach licorice-scented star anise to a fabric-covered wreath.

POCKET POTPOURRIS, JAR COVERS, AND WREATH

§

• **MATERIALS**

Plaid fabric, decorative cord, pinking shears, plastic foam wreath form, star anise, straight pins, potpourri.

BOWS AND JAR LID

Cut pieces of fabric to desired size and tie as shown in photo.

CAT AND HEART

Cut 2 pieces of fabric with pattern as a guide, adding 1/4" (1 cm) seam allowance. With right sides together, sew around edge, leaving an opening for stuffing. Trim corners, turn right side out, and stuff with potpourri. Sew the opening closed. Tie cord around the cat's neck.

POCKET POTPOURRIS

Cut fabric rectangles the desired size and sew together, leaving top open. Fill with potpourri. Fold top edges to outside as shown in photo. Tie cord under the cuff.

WREATH

Cut fabric in strips and wrap around foam form as shown in photo. Pin star anise around the wreath in a decorative pattern. ■

Patterns at right shown at 80% of actual size. Photocopy at 125%.

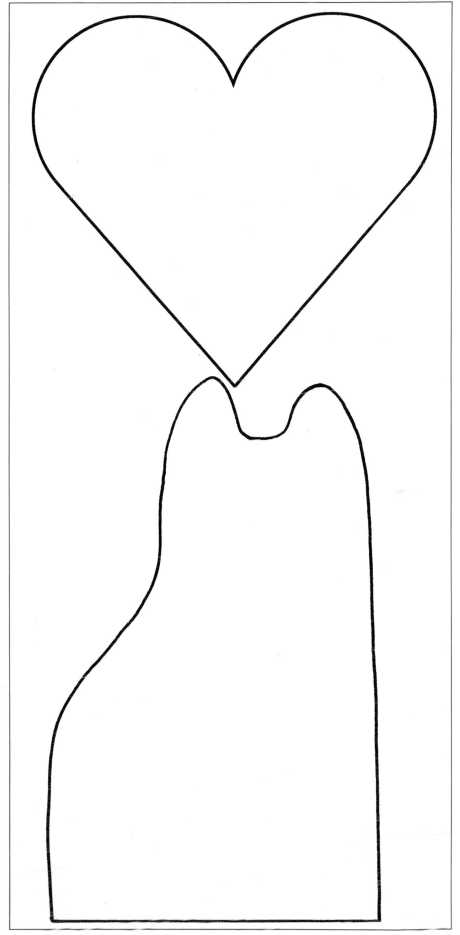

RED & ECRU KITCHEN

············ ∾ ············

Red and white checked fabric is a classic country touch. The projects on these pages update that look with a somewhat subtler fabric and a dressier style. There are gracefully draped curtains with decorative bands (page 88), napkins with contrasting trim (page 88), covered pillows with accenting bows (page 90), and a fabric-covered recipe holder (page 90) to hold all those odd-sized recipes you've clipped from various magazines over the last 15 years.

CURTAINS WITH DECORATIVE BANDS

∽

• **MATERIALS**

Red/ecru checked fabric, 16" (40 cm) hook and loop tape, thread.

• **INSTRUCTIONS**

Measure the window from the outer edges of the frame. Allow enough fabric for these measurements plus 1-1/2" (4 cm) extra in width and 5-1/2" (14 cm) extra in length. For the front bands, cut 2 strips 8-3/4" (22 cm) wide and the length of the curtain plus 6" (15 cm). For back bands, cut 2 strips 8-3/4" (22 cm) wide and the length of the curtain plus 1/4" (1 cm).

Hem sides of the curtain: press edges to wrong side 1/2" (2 cm), then fold raw edges under and stitch. For top and bottom hems, turn under 2-3/4" (7 cm) at each end, turn under raw edges 1/4" (1 cm), press and stitch.

To make bands, sew each front band section to a back band section across one end with 1/4" (1 cm) seam allowance. Fold each piece in half lengthwise, right sides together, and stitch the long raw edges together with 1/4" (1 cm) seam allowance. Turn bands right side out through the open ends and fold so seam is at center of the back. Sew remaining (top) ends of bands together. Position the curtain within the bands with the outer edges of bands evenly spaced from sides of the curtain. Place end seams of bands at top of curtain so front bands are longer than back bands. Stitch bands in place along upper hemline of curtain.

Determine length to which curtain will hang, and accordion pleat lower

end of curtain to this length. Cut hook and loop tape into 4 strips, positioning strips on inside of front and back bands to hold curtain at desired length. ∎

NAPKINS WITH CONTRASTING TRIM AND BOWS

∽

• **FINISHED MEASUREMENTS**

16-1/4" (41 cm) square.

• **MATERIALS**

For 6 napkins: beige/ecru striped cotton, 1 yd. (.8 m) 56" (140 cm) wide or 1-1/2 yds (1.4 m) 45" (115 cm) wide. Red/ecru checked cotton, 3/4 yd (.6 m) 45" or 56" (115 cm or 140 cm) wide. Ecru thread, paper, ruler, pencil.

• **INSTRUCTIONS**

For each napkin, cut a 16" (40 cm) square from striped fabric. Make a paper pattern 1-1/4" x 17" (3.5 cm x 42.5 cm). Fold in half lengthwise. Cut ends diagonally at a 45° angle so that the folded edge is 17" (42.5 cm) long and the cut edges are 15-1/2" (39 cm) long. Make a second paper pattern 1-1/4" x 26" (3.5 cm x 65 cm), folding lengthwise and angling corners as before. Open the patterns and pin to doubled checked fabric. Add 1/4" (1 cm) seam allowance and cut 2 trim strips from each pattern for each napkin.

With right sides together, sew the 2 shorter strips to 2 adjacent sides of the napkin with a 1/4" (1 cm) seam, beginning and ending the stitching 1/4" (1 cm) from the edges of the napkin. Fold the napkin diagonally and stitch the ends of the trim together at the corner, beginning and ending 1/4" (1 cm) from the edges and pivoting at the point. Stitch one end of each long trim strip to the end of one strip end on the napkin as above, so that the trim extensions are on adjacent corners of the napkins. Then sew the long edges of the trim strips to the napkin edges. Press as before. Trim corners close to stitching, and turn right

side out. Turn raw edges under to just cover stitching line, and press. Turn in seam allowances on trim extensions and press. Slipstitch or machine stitch in place. Tie bows with the trim extensions. ■

PILLOW COVER WITH BOWS

- **FINISHED MEASUREMENTS**
16" x 16" (40 cm x 40 cm).

- **MATERIALS**
1 yd (.8 m) red/ecru checked cotton 45" or 56" (115 cm or 140 cm) wide, 12" (30 cm) zipper, ecru thread, pillow form 16" x 16" (40 cm x 40 cm).

- **INSTRUCTIONS**
For cushion front, cut a 25" (38 cm) square from one corner of the checked fabric. From the corner diagonally opposite, cut 2 pieces 8" x 15" (20.5 cm x 38 cm) for the back. Cut 4 bias strips 2" (5 cm) wide and about 35" (89 cm) long. With right sides together and 1/2" (1.5 cm) seam allowance, stitch back sections together 1-1/2" (4 cm) from each end. Machine baste remainder of seam. Press seam open, place zipper

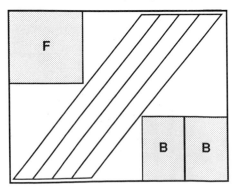

Pillow Cover with Bows Layout

over basted portion of seam, and stitch it in place.

Mark centers of 4 sides of pillow front and of 4 bias strips. Matching centers, sew a strip to each side of pillow front with right sides together and 1/4" (1 cm) seam allowance. Sew back to strips in the same manner. Hem remaining long edges and ends of strips with a single 1/4" (1 cm) hem. Turn the cover right side out and insert pillow form. Tie bows at the corners. ■

RECIPE HOLDER

(See photo on page 89.)

- **MATERIALS**
A purchased magazine holder made of cardboard or book board, beige/white fabric, red/ecru checked fabric, fusible interfacing, white glue, paper, felt-tip marker

- **INSTRUCTIONS**
Measure the outside dimensions of the magazine holder and cut out a piece of beige/white fabric large enough to cover the box, adding about an inch (2.5 cm) to the height and the circumference. Measure the inside dimensions of the file folder. Cut a piece of the fabric long enough to wrap around the walls, and a piece to fit the bottom.

Fuse interfacing to the wrong side of the fabric. Fold fabric around box, overlapping the cut ends about an inch (2.5 cm) and folding an inch of extra fabric over the top. Glue in place. Glue fabric to the inside surfaces, trimming the wall panels even with the top edge. Let dry.

Cut a rectangle from red/ecru fabric and a smaller paper rectangle, and trim the corners diagonally. Label the holder. ■

PUFFY CURTAIN

෴

- **MATERIALS**

Yellow/white striped cotton fabric, ring tape, curtain cord, pleater tape, strip of wood 1" x 2" (2.5 cm x 5 cm) cut 1" (3 cm) shorter than finished width of curtain, 4 screw eyes 3/4" (2 cm) diameter, 2 mounting brackets, small awning cleat, paint or small squares of curtain fabric.

- **INSTRUCTIONS**

Measure the width of window and frame. Make finished curtain 1/2" (1.5 cm) wider than this measurement at each side. Allow 1-1/2 times this measurement for pleats. If necessary, piece the fabric to obtain desired width. Measure the length of the window and frame, and add 1-1/2" (4 cm) for hems. Make a narrow double hem on each side and a 1" (3 cm) double hem at the lower edge of the curtain. Make a 1/2" (1 cm) single hem across the upper edge.

Sew pleater tape to the top of the curtain, placing the upper edge of the tape 1/8" (.5 cm) below the upper edge of the curtain and turning under the ends even with side hems. Stitch around all 4 edges of the tape. Place 4 strips of ring tape on the wrong side of the curtain, with the lower ring of each strip 1/4" (1 cm) above the hem and the upper ends at the bottom of the pleater tape. Place outer edges of the 2 outer strips at the side hemlines and space the 2 inner strips evenly between them. Stitch along both edges of the tape strips and across the ends. Pleat the top of the curtain to the desired finished width and stitch pleats in place.

Paint the ends of the wood strip to match window trim or glue squares of curtain fabric over them. Position the curtain along the wood strip, with the sides of the curtain extending 1/2" (1.5 cm) beyond the ends of the strip. Attach 4 screw eyes along a narrow side of the wood strip, placing one directly above each ring strip on the curtain. Tack curtain to front of strip, with upper edge of curtain about 1/4" (1 cm) above top of strip. Attach a bracket at each side of upper window trim, inside placement point for outer eyes on wood strip.

Determine whether curtain cord should hang to right or left. Attach cleat to lower part of window frame on that side. Beginning at the opposite side of the curtain, knot a piece of cord to the lower ring on the tape. String the cord upward through the remaining rings on the tape and across through the eyes on the wood strip, allowing enough extra cord to hang about 6" (15 cm) below bottom of curtain. Repeat, with 1 piece of cord for each strip of ring tape on the curtain. Braid loose ends of cord together. Hang wood strip on mounting brackets. Wind braided cord around cleat to secure curtain at desired height. ∎

SMOCKED SHELF EDGING

෴

(See photo on page 94.)

- **FINISHED MEASUREMENTS**

1-1/4" (3.5 cm) wide.

- **MATERIALS**

A strip of striped cotton 3" (7.5 cm) wide and about 3 times the desired finished length, blue and white embroidery floss, white sewing thread, ruler, pencil.

- **INSTRUCTIONS**

Make a 1/4" (1 cm) hem along 1 long edge for lower edge. Zigzag stitch along upper edge. With pencil, mark 3 lines 1/8" (3 mm) apart, placing the first line 3/4" (2 cm) from the lower edge. Fold the upper edge 1" (2.5 cm) to wrong side of work. Work a rolled hem on the left edge by overcasting with a short, narrow zigzag stitch. Using 2 strands of floss, smock at stripes. Begin at left edge. Make first stitch above and below the top line. Make the second and third stitches above and below the center and lower lines. Smock the desired length, following the step by step instructions. Stitch between the stitches, working under the center stitches as shown in photo. Work a rolled hem on the right edge.

ENGLISH SMOCKING STEP BY STEP

1. Beginning at left edge at top line, skip 2 stripes. Whipstitch over 2 stripes as shown in photo, working from left to right and gathering stripes.

2. Beginning at lower line, make a second stitch by inserting needle at the next stripe and the second stripe of the first stitch as shown in photo.

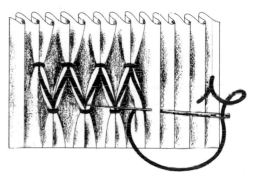

3. Complete the stitch as before.

4. Insert the needle in the lower row at the next stripe and the second stripe of the previous stitch and continue to desired length.

Not wor sam gat! firs

CHAIR COVERS WITH LACED BACKS
↬

• MATERIALS
Ivory brocade cotton, fusible interfacing, ecru crochet cotton #8, cording, craft knife, tracing paper, pins.

• INSTRUCTIONS
Measure the chair back from top to floor and from top to seat. Measure the seat and front. For the back laced

panel, measure the back and add 11" (28 cm) at center back for the box pleat. Make paper patterns for all pieces, adding 1/2" (1.5 cm) seam allowance and 2-1/4" (5.5 cm) hems. Cut out the pieces. For piping, cut a strip of fabric twice the depth of the chair seat, plus the width across the front, plus 1" (3 cm). Note: sew all pieces with right sides together and with 1/2" (1.5 cm) seam allowance.

MAKE THE BACK

Mark center back and mark a point 5-1/2" (14 cm) from center on each side. Bring the side marks to center to form a box pleat. Press folds flat. Mark 3 or more 1/2" (1.5 cm) circles on each side of pleat about 1-1/4" (3.5 cm) from folds and 4" (10 cm) apart. Fuse a strip of interfacing to back of each pleat behind the circles. Cut out the circles, cutting through only the top two layers that form the pleat. With crochet thread, work buttonhole stitch around each circle.

MAKE PIPING

Fold the fabric strip in half, lengthwise, *right side out*. Place cord in the fold and stitch fabric layers together, using a zipper foot to sew as closely to the cord as possible. Sew piping around sides and front of seat, keeping stitching line of piping on the seamline. Clip the piping to stitching at corner.

ASSEMBLE THE COVER

Sew the seat with piping to front of seat back. Sew sides to lower front piece, then sew this piece to seat. Sew on back piece.

Press a 2-1/4" (5.5 cm) hem

around the bottom. Fold the raw edge under 1/4" (1 cm) and stitch. For laces, cut 2 fabric strips 2-1/2" x 46" (6 cm x 115 cm). Fold strips in half lengthwise with right sides together and stitch long edges, leaving ends open. Turn right side out. Sew the pieces together at one end. Turn the other ends to inside and stitch. Fold in half lengthwise and lace through back. ■

RUFFLED PICTURE FRAMES

• MATERIALS

For each picture: mat board 7" x 9-1/2" (18 cm x 24 cm), print fabric 14-1/4" x 19-1/4" (36 cm x 48 cm), pinking shears, thread, pencil, tape, cardboard 7" x 9-1/2" (18 cm x 24 cm), a picture.

• INSTRUCTIONS

Draw a rectangle 9-1/4" x 14" (23 cm x 35 cm) in the center of the fabric. Draw a second rectangle 3/4" (2 cm) inside the first, and cut out the inner rectangle. Trim around the outside of fabric with pinking shears. Sew around the inner edges with a basting stitch and gather fabric to make a finished rectangle about 11" x 13-1/2" (28 cm x 34 cm). Tape the inner edges of the fabric to the back of the mat board so that the outer border is 2-1/2" (5 cm) wide. Glue the mat board to the cardboard. Glue the picture in place. ■

PINK & WHITE STRIPED BEDROOM

.... ꋖ ....

Country bedrooms may be done in bright primary colors or in pastel hues, but consistently they speak of comfort, relaxation, and warmth. Often considered nursery colors, pink and white can offer a very adult sophis-lication, especially when paired with rich wood tones.

Projects in this room include a striped bedspread and set of pillowcases that can be neatly folded and tied, as shown in the photo above. There's a series of accent pillows (page 100), ruffled curtains with stenciled tiebacks (page 102), a sleek bed skirt with corner bows (page 104), and a pique cushion for a wooden chair (page 105).

STRIPED BEDSPREAD AND MATCHING PILLOWCASES

⟡

• FINISHED MEASUREMENTS

Bedspread 80" (202 cm) square (double bed size), pillowcases 23" x 28" (60 cm x 72 cm).

• MATERIALS

For bedspread, 9-1/2 yds (8.7 m) pink/white striped cotton fabric 48" (122 cm) wide. For 2 pillowcases, 2-1/2 yds (2 m) of the same fabric. Thread.

• INSTRUCTIONS

Cut all pieces with the stripes going lengthwise. Match stripes wherever possible. Cut 2 pieces 48" x 81" (120 cm x 205 cm) and 4 pieces 17-1/2" x 81" (44 cm x 205 cm) for the bedspread front and back. For the flap, cut 2 pieces 9-1/2" x 81" (23 cm x 205 cm). For ties, cut 16 strips 1-3/4" x 19" (4.5 cm x 48 cm). For the pillowcases, cut 2 pieces 29" x 48" (74 cm x 122 cm). For the flaps, cut 4 strips 9-1/2" x 25" (23 cm x 63 cm). For ties, cut 16 strips 1-3/4" x 14" (4.5 cm x 36 cm). Sew all pieces with right sides together and 1/2" (1.5 cm) seam allowance except where otherwise noted.

BEDSPREAD

For the bedspread front, sew one of the narrow pieces to each side of the large piece along the long edges. Repeat for the back. Hem one long edge of each flap piece with 1/2" (1.5 cm) double hems.

Fold the tie strips in half lengthwise and sew the long edges and across one end of each. Trim corners and turn right side out. Position 8 ties across the lower edge of the bedspread front, spacing them evenly along the edge. Pin them in place with the unfinished ends even with the edge of the spread. Repeat for the back, placing the ties opposite those on the front. Stitch the unhemmed long edges of the flap pieces to the lower edges of the spread front and back. Sew the front and back together around 3 unfinished edges, stitching the flap front and back together at the same time. Trim corners and turn right side out. Turn flap to inside along seamline; press. Topstitch around the opening 1/2" (1.5 cm) from the folded edge. Put a blanket inside the cover if desired, and tie the ties.

PILLOWCASES

Make ties as for the bedspread. Position the ties along one long edge of the pillowcase so that when the piece is folded in half the ties will lie opposite each other in pairs. Pin them in place.

Stitch 2 flap pieces together at one end. Make a 1/2" (1.5 cm) double hem on one long edge. Stitch the flap to the case. Fold the piece in half and sew the case and ends of the flap together along the 2 edges. Clip corners, turn, and topstitch as for the bedspread. Insert the pillow and tie the ties. ∎

STENCILED PILLOW

⟡

(Opposite page, far left.)

• FINISHED MEASUREMENTS

18" x 18" x 2-1/2" (45 cm x 45 cm x 6.5 cm).

• MATERIALS

5/8 yd (.6 m) white cotton fabric 45" (115 cm) wide, 5/8 yd (.6 m) floral print cotton fabric 45" (115 cm) wide, thread, fusible interfacing, zipper 12" (30 cm) long, dressmakers' carbon, stenciling acetate, craft knife, stenciling brush, fabric paint: light pink, pink, dark red, and green, or to match colors of fabric.

• INSTRUCTIONS

From white fabric, cut a piece 19" (48 cm) square for the front. Cut a piece 19" x 17" (48 cm x 44 cm) and a piece 19" x 3" (48 cm x 8 cm) for the back. From the floral print, cut 2 squares 8-1/2" (22 cm) on a side, and 4 strips 3" x 36" (8 cm x 92 cm). Cut 2 squares of

Stencil Pattern for Pillow.
Shown 75% of actual size.
Photocopy at 133%.

interfacing 8" (20 cm) on a side.

Place the 2 back pieces together along a 19" (48 cm) side. With right sides together and 1/2" (1.5 cm) seam allowance, stitch 3" (7.5 cm) from each end toward center and machine baste the rest of the seam. Press seam open. Center the zipper, face down, over the basted section of the seam on the wrong side. Stitch in place.

Center the interfacing squares on the wrong side of the floral print squares and fuse in place. Turn under the edges of the print squares, creasing them at the edges of the interfacing. Press in place. Center the floral squares on the front and back pieces, angling them so that the corners of each square point to the centers of the edges. Sew in place, stitching very close to the edges of the squares.

Make a full-size paper pattern of the stencil motif. Trace it onto a corner of the acetate 1-1/2" (4 cm) inside the edges. Cut out the design areas. Position the stencil on a corner of the pillow front, aligning the edges. Paint the flowers light pink, the centers dark red, the leaves green, and the curved lines pink. Hold the brush vertically to paint, and remove excess paint from the brush onto scrap paper. Stencil the design on each corner of the pillow front. Heat-set the paint according to the manufacturer's instructions.

Mark the center of each edge of the pillow front and back and of each fabric strip. Sew a strip to each edge of the pillow front, with right sides together and 1/2" (1.5 cm) seam allowance, matching centers. Begin and end stitching 1/2" (1.5 cm) from the corners of the pillow front. Sew the pillow back to the strips in the same way. Turn the cover right side out. Fold the ends of the strips in half lengthwise, with right sides together. Mark a point 3" (8 cm) from the end

of the strip, on the seamline. Using 1/4" (1 cm) seam allowance, begin stitching as closely as possible to the corner of the pillow. When the marked point is reached, stitch on the diagonal across the end to the seamline at the opposite corner. Trim corners and trim to 1/8" (.5 cm) from the diagonal stitching line. Turn the ties right side out. Insert the pillow form in the cover and knot the ties at the corners.

For a variation of this pillow, use floral print for the pillow front and back, with a floral motif appliqued on a white fabric circle and centered on the front. Or use the pattern shown below to cut pieces for a floral star to applique to a white pillow front. Or make a shirred edge strip by cutting the strip 1-1/2 times the pillow circumference then gathering it to fit the front and back. ■

RUFFLED CURTAINS WITH STENCILED TIEBACKS

∽

• **MATERIALS**
For the curtain, floral print cotton fabric and white cotton fabric. For 2 ties, 3/4 yd (.7 m) white cotton fabric 60" (150 cm) wide, 3/4 yd (.7 m) floral print cotton fabric 60" (150 cm) wide, dressmakers' carbon, stenciling acetate, stenciling brush, craft knife, 2 screw hooks, 4 curtain rings 3/4" (2 cm) in diameter, fabric paints: red, white, green and black.

• **INSTRUCTIONS**
Measure the width of the window and frame, and the length from the rod to the floor. For each curtain of the pair, allow twice the width of the window for pleats and side hems. To the length measurement add 8" (20 cm) for hems. Cut the 2 curtains. Cut white fabric for 2 ruffles, each 1-1/2 times the curtain length and 8-3/4" (22 cm) wide.

Stitch a 1/2" (1.5 cm) double hem along the *outer* long edge of each curtain. Stitch a 5" (13 cm) double hem at the lower edge. Stitch a 3" (7 cm) double hem along the top, or hem the top according to the kind of rod that will be used.

Stitch narrow double hems along the short ends of the ruffles. Fold a ruffle piece in half, right side out, and sew the long edges together with 2 rows of machine basting, inside and outside the seamline. Gather the ruffle to fit the length of the curtain. Pin each ruffle to an inner (un-

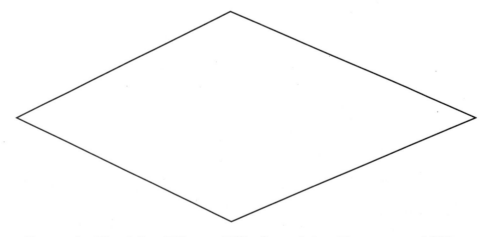

Pattern for Floral Star Pillow at 75% of actual size. Photocopy at 133%.

Stencil Pattern for Tieback.
Shown at 75% of actual size.
Photocopy at 133%.

hemmed) edge of the curtain, with right sides together, and stitch.

Make a full-size paper pattern for the tieback. Cut 4 pieces from folded fabric with no added seam allowance. Cut strips of floral print fabric:
2 strips 2" x 26-1/4" (5 cm x 66 cm),
2 strips 2" x 24" (5 cm x 60 cm), and
4 strips 2" x 4" (5 cm x 10 cm).

Make a full-size drawing of the floral motif and trace it onto acetate. Cut out the design areas. Stencil the design on 2 tieback pieces, placing the M of the motif at precisely the center of the fabric. Wipe excess paint from the brush before painting on the fabric, and hold the brush vertically to keep the bristles from slipping under the acetate. Paint the flowers light pink (mix white and a little red), the flower centers dark red (mix red with black), the leaves light green (mix green and white), and the curved lines rose (mix red

and a little white). Turn the stencil over to paint a mirror image of the design on the second piece, as in the photo. Set the paint according to the manufacturer's instructions.

Place a painted and a plain tie section with wrong sides together and bind the edges with strips of floral fabric. Bind a long edge first, and end with a short side. First sew the strip to the back of the tie, with right sides together and 1/4" (1 cm) seam allowance. Double the remainder of the strip and fold over the edge so it just covers the previous stitching line. Stitch close to the edge of the trim on the front side.

Sew a ring to each end of each tieback 1/2" (1.5 cm) from the top. Attach a hook to the window frame at the desired height. Wrap the tiebacks around the curtains and slip rings over the hooks. ∎

BED SKIRT WITH
CORNER BOWS

∾

• **MATERIALS**

Heavy white cotton fabric and
lighter weight white cotton fabric
56" (140 cm) wide for the bed skirt.
For 2 bows, 3/4 yd (.6 m) white
cotton fabric 56" (140 cm) wide.

• **INSTRUCTIONS**

Measure the length of the bed from

head to foot plus the height from
the box spring to the floor, and add
1" (3 cm) at each end for hems.
Measure the width of the bed from
the floor over the box spring to the
floor, and add 1" (3 cm) to each side
for hems. Cut the heavy fabric to
these measurements. If necessary,
seam 2 pieces at center to get the
necessary width.

For the lining, cut the lighter cotton
fabric to the same measurements.
Place the 2 pieces with right sides
together and stitch around the
edges, leaving an opening on one
side for turning. Trim the corners,

turn right side out, and stitch across
the opening.

For the bows, cut 2 strips 10" x
52-1/4" (25 cm x 131 cm). Fold the
strips in half lengthwise, with right
sides together. Stitch the ends and
long edge with 1/8" (.5 cm) seam
allowance, leaving an opening at the
center of the long edge for turning.
Trim the corners, turn right side
out, and stitch across the opening.

Place the bed skirt over the box
spring. Fold the fabric at the
corners as shown in the photo. Tie
the bows and stitch them to the
corners. ∎

PIQUE CHAIR CUSHION

෴

• MATERIALS

White cotton pique, thick fiberfill batting, white thread.

• INSTRUCTIONS

Make a paper pattern of the chair seat, adding 1/2" (1.5 cm) seam allowance all around. Cut out around the back spindles if necessary, and round the front corners slightly. Cut 2 pieces from fabric and one piece from batting. For the ruffles, measure the distance between the back spindles, and measure the distance around the sides and across the front. For each of these measurements, cut 2 strips twice the measurement plus about 2" (5 cm) for each corner, and 8-3/4" (22 cm) wide. For the ties, cut 4 strips 2" x 34" (5 cm x 85 cm).

Fold the ruffle strips in half lengthwise, with right sides together, and stitch the ends. Turn right side out. Machine baste the long edges of each strip together with 2 rows of machine basting, inside and outside the seamline. Gather the pieces to fit the top of the chair cushion and pin to the right side of the top, matching raw edges.

Fold each tie strip in half lengthwise, wrong side out. Stitch the long edges together and stitch diagonally across one end. Trim the corners and turn right side out. Pin one tie to each back corner of the chair cushion top, between the top and the ruffle, the end of the tie even with the edge of the cushion. Pin one tie to each side/back corner in the same way. Stitch the ruffle and ties to the cushion top.

Baste the batting to the wrong side of the cushion bottom. Pin the bottom to the top with right sides together and stitch, leaving about 10" (25 cm) open along the back for turning. Trim the batting close to the stitching, and trim seams and corners. Turn right side out and stitch across the opening. Place the cushion on its chair, wrap the ties around the legs as shown in the photo, and tie the ends. ∎

FRILLY COUNTRY BED LINEN

.... §§ ....

If you're fortunate enough to own a handsome antique bed, you'll want bed linens that are worthy of it. A ruffled duvet cover and eyelet-trimmed pillowcases will draw all eyes to the bed without hiding its good looks. Purchase a few extra pillows and an embroidered throw, for an even more distinguished setting.

Ruffled Duvet Cover

⌖

(See photo on page 106.)

- **Finished Measurements**

68" x 86" (172 cm x 213 cm), excluding ruffle, to fit a twin-size comforter.

- **Materials**

9-1/4 yds (8.4 m) floral print fabric 54" (137 cm) wide, thread.

- **Instructions**

Cut a piece of fabric 54" x 86" (137 cm x 218 cm) for the front, a piece 54" x 84-1/2" (137 cm x 214 cm) for the back, and a piece 54" x 7-1/2" (137 cm x 19 cm) for the back flap. On the lengthwise grain, cut 2 pieces 8-1/2" x 86" (22 cm x 218 cm), 2 pieces 8-1/2" x 84-1/2" (22 cm x 214 cm), and 2 pieces 8-1/2" x 7-1/2" (22 cm x 19 cm). Sew one strip of each pair to each side of the larger piece the same length, with right sides together and 1/2" (1.5 cm) seam allowance, so that the 3 cover pieces are 69" (175 cm) wide.

For the ruffle, cut 6 strips 8-3/4" x 54" (22 cm x 137 cm). Sew the ends with right sides together and 1/4" (1 cm) seam allowance to form a large ring. Fold in half, right side out, and stitch the raw edges together with 2 rows of long machine stitch, breaking the stitching at about 8 points around the ruffle. Gather the ruffle to fit the top piece and stitch to the right side of the piece with raw edges together and 1/4" (1 cm) seam allowance.

Hem one 69" (175 cm) side of each back piece with a 1" (3 cm) double hem. Place the front piece right side up. Place the small back flap on top,

wrong side up, aligning the raw edges. Place the large back piece on top of these, wrong side up, aligning the raw edges. Stitch around the edges with 1/2" (1.5 cm) seam allowance. Trim corners and turn right side out. Insert the comforter. ∎

Eyelet-Trimmed Pillowcase

⌖

- **Finished Measurements**

21" x 29" (56 cm x 74 cm), excluding trim.

- **Materials**

One yard (.9 m) printed cotton fabric 45" (115 cm) wide, 5-1/2 yds (5 m) white eyelet edging 2-3/4" (7 cm) wide, pillow 19" x 26" (48 cm x 66 cm), thread.

- **Instructions**

Cut a piece of fabric 22" x 29" (56 cm x 74 cm) for the front. Cut a piece 22" x 15-1/2" (56 cm x 40 cm) and a piece 22" x 17-1/2" (56 cm x 45 cm) for the back.

Sew the narrow ends of the eyelet together to form a ring. Gather the unfinished edge to fit around the edge of the pillowcase front. Pin to the right side of the front with raw edges together and stitch in place with 1/4" (1 cm) seam allowance.

Hem one long edge of each back piece with a 1" (3 cm) double hem. Place the front piece right side up. Place the smaller back piece on it, wrong side up, with the raw edges together. On top of these 2, place the larger back piece, wrong side up, aligning the raw edges. Stitch around all edges. Trim the corners and turn right side out. Insert the pillow. ∎

STRIPED BEDSPREAD AND PILLOWCASE

∽

• **FINISHED MEASUREMENTS**

Bedspread, 83" x 82" (211 cm x 205.5 cm), double bed size. Pillowcases, 26" x 32-1/4" (65.5 cm x 81 cm).

• **MATERIALS**

For bedspread and 2 pillowcases, 11-3/4 yds (10.8 m) beige/white striped cotton fabric 56" (140 cm) wide, beige thread.

• **INSTRUCTIONS**

Match the stripes at seamlines wherever possible. For backing, cut one piece 56" x 83-3/4" (140 cm x 209.5 cm) and 2 pieces 15" x 83-3/4" (38.5 cm x 209.5 cm). For the top, cut one piece 56" x 83" (140 cm x 207.5 cm) and 2 pieces 15" x 83" (38.5 cm x 207.5 cm). For the flap, cut one piece 9-1/2" x 84" (24 cm x 213 cm). For the pillowcases, cut 2 pieces for the fronts, 27" x 33-1/4" (67.5 cm x 83 cm), for the backs, cut 2 pieces 27-3/4" x 33 1/4" (69.5 cm x 83 cm), and for the flaps cut 2 pieces 9-1/2" x 33-1/4" (24 cm x 83 cm). Sew all pieces with right sides together and with 1/2" (1 cm seam allowance.

BEDSPREAD

For the backing, sew a narrow piece to each side of the large piece so that the backing is 84" (213 cm) wide. Stitch a 1-1/4" (3 cm) double hem along the lower edge. Sew the side front pieces to the center front piece. Hem one long edge of the flap with a narrow double hem. Sew the unhemmed edge of the flap to the lower edge of the front. Fold the flap to the wrong side of the front.

Pin the back and front together, and stitch around the 3 unfinished sides, sewing the flap ends into the seam. Trim corners and turn right side out. Place a blanket inside the cover if desired.

To form the borders, stitch along the sides and top, through both thicknesses, with a fairly close zigzag stitch a scant 1/8" (4 mm) wide. Place the stitching line 2-1/4" (5.5 cm) from the edge.

PILLOWCASES

This pillowcase is open on a long edge rather than on an end. Hem one long edge of the flap with a narrow double hem. Stitch the unhemmed long edge to the long edge of the pillowcase front. Turn the flap to the wrong side of the front.

Stitch a 1-1/4" (3 cm) double hem along one long edge of the pillowcase back. Pin the front to the back along the 3 unfinished edges; stitch. Trim corners and turn right side out. Stitch the border as for the bedspread. ■

PLEATED TABLE SKIRT

∽

• **FINISHED MEASUREMENTS**

28" (70 cm) diameter, for a table 30" high.

• **MATERIALS**

White linen or cotton, 7/8 yd (.9 m), 3-1/2 yds (3.2 m) beige/white cotton 56" (140 cm) wide, with 2-1/4" (5.5 cm) stripes, white thread.

• **INSTRUCTIONS**

From the white fabric cut a circle 28-3/4" (72 cm) in diameter. From striped fabric, cut 3 pieces 31" x 53-1/2" (78 cm x 134 cm), and one piece 31" x 20-1/2" (78 cm x 51.5 cm). Cut the striped pieces with the edge of the beige stripe on the seamline, and the 3/8" (1 cm) seam allowance on the white stripe.

With right sides together, sew the striped pieces together along the 31" (78 cm) sides. Stitch a 1/2" (1.5 cm) double hem around the lower edge. Fold pleats around the upper edge so that only the white stripes show on the outside, as in the photo. Stitch the pleats in place along the seamline.

Machine stitch around the outer edge of the white circle 3/8" (1 cm) from the edge. Turn under the edge at the stitching line; press. Pin the right side of the pleated skirt to the wrong side of the top with a 3/4" (2 cm) overlap. Stitch in place, stitching close to the edge of the circle. Stitch around the circle again, 1/4" (1 cm) inside the first stitching line. ■

WINTER BLANKET

↭

• **FINISHED MEASUREMENTS**
90" (230 cm) square.

• **MATERIALS**
Cotton print fabric, 8 yds (7.3 m) at 45" (115 cm) wide or 6-1/2 yds (6 m) at 54" wide. Cotton fabric for the backing, 5-1/4 yds (4.8 m) 45" (115 cm) wide, and 5-1/2 yds (5 m) heavy white cotton flannel 45" (115 cm) wide.

• **INSTRUCTIONS**

Preshrink all fabrics before cutting. Sew all pieces with right sides together and with 1/4" (1 cm) seam allowance.

From the cotton print, cut 8 blocks 19-1/2" x 39" (50 cm x 98 cm). For the borders, cut 12 strips 12-1/2" x 30-1/4" (31.5 cm x 76.5 cm). Sew the long edges of 4 blocks together to form 2 strips of 4 blocks each. Sew these together along one long edge. Sew 3 strips together to make 1 strip 90-3/4" (229.5 cm) long. Make a total of 4 long strips. Press the strips in half lengthwise with wrong sides together. Mark the center of the long edge of each strip.

Sew the border strips to the pieced front, matching centers. Begin and end the stitching lines 1/4" (1 cm) from the ends of the front piece. Miter the corners: at each corner, stitch border strips together from the ends of the previous stitching lines to the lengthwise crease at a 45-degree angle, so that the corner will lie flat.

Cut the flannel in half, crosswise. Sew the pieces together along one long edge and trim ends to form a piece 89" (226 cm) square. Clip selvages. Repeat with the cotton fabric. Stitch the flannel to the wrong side of the cotton around the edges. Mark the center of each side.

Place the flannel side of the backing against the wrong side of the pieced front, matching centers, so that the backing lies within the pressed creases of the border. Fold borders to inside, and fold under the raw edge 1/4" (1 cm), just over the previous stitching line. Press. Miter the inside corners by folding at a 45-degree angle to match the outer corners. Trim away excess fabric at corners and press. Stitch in place. Stitch around the edges of the border, close to the fold. Topstitch 1" (3 cm) from outer edges. ■

FARM SCENE BEDROOM

.... ℘ ....

Nothing says "country" like cows. Only lately have we discovered that these rather bulky animals are interesting-looking. For a bedroom with a rural scene, make a black and white holstein-patterned bedspread lined in bright green, red, and blue (page 116). Follow the gridded pattern, or adapt the markings to match the cow of your choice. For another bright spot of color, make a curtain tieback with appliqued barn and trees (page 118).

HOLSTEIN BEDSPREAD

〰

- **FINISHED MEASUREMENTS**

55" x 79" (136 cm x 197 cm).

- **MATERIALS**

3 yds (2.6 m) white cotton fabric 60" (150 cm) wide, 4-1/2 yds (4.2 m) green cotton fabric 45" (115 cm) wide, 2-1/2 yds (2.2 m) black cotton fabric 45" (115 cm) wide, 3/4 yd (.7 m) blue cotton fabric 45" (115 cm) wide, 1/4 yd (.3 m) red cotton fabric 45" (115 cm) wide. Black, green, blue, red, and white thread. Kraft paper, glue stick, rotary cutter and mat or sharp scissors.

- **INSTRUCTIONS**

For the top, cut a piece of white cotton fabric 56" x 80" (140 cm x 200 cm). Cut black cow spots according to the chart. Position them on the white fabric and use the glue stick to hold them in place. With black thread, stitch around the motifs with a zigzag stitch, overcasting the edges.

For the backing, cut a piece of green fabric 80" (200 cm) long and 45" (115 cm) wide. Cut 2 strips 6-1/2" x 80" (15.5 cm x 200 cm). Stitch one strip to each long side of the large green piece with right sides together and 1/2" (1.5 cm) seam allowance.

From heavy paper, cut 2 squares 8" (20 cm) on a side. Fold one square in half diagonally and cut along the fold to make 2 triangles. Cut 8 triangles from red fabric. Cut 12 squares from white fabric. Cut the blue fabric into strips 11" (28 cm) wide and piece them as necessary to make 2 strips 56" (140 cm) long. Cut 8 cowlike

spots from black fabric and applique them onto the white squares.

Following the diagram, position the red, blue, and white pieces on the right side of the backing. Dot with glue to hold them in place. Stitch around the edges of each piece with a zigzag stitch, using thread to match the piece. Trim the ends of

the blue strip even with the backing.

With right sides together and 1/2" (1.5 cm) seam allowance, sew the top to the backing around all edges, leaving an opening of about 24" (60 cm) along the bottom edge for turning. Clip corners and turn right side out. Stitch across the opening. ∎

Above: Layout of Holstein Spots. Right: Bedspread Lining.

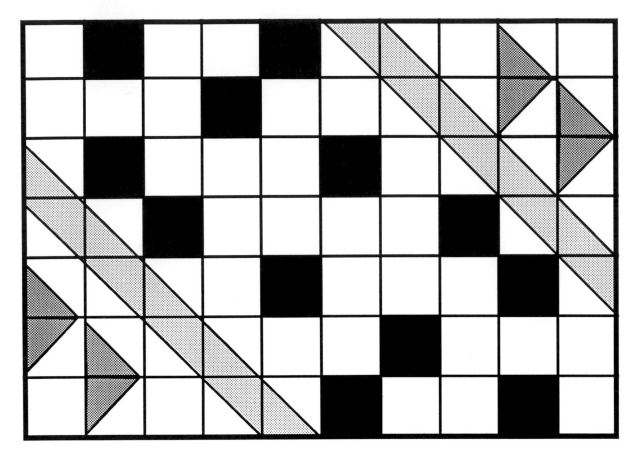

CURTAIN TIEBACK WITH FARM SCENE

❧

• **FINISHED MEASUREMENTS**

3-3/4" x 29" (9 cm x 73 cm).

• **MATERIALS**

For one tieback: a strip of green cotton fabric 1-1/2" x 29-1/2" (4 cm x 74 cm), a strip of blue cotton fabric 6-1/4" x 29-1/2" (16 cm x 74 cm), small pieces of cotton fabric in green, dark green, red, white, and blue. Thread to match fabrics, kraft paper, dressmakers' carbon, paper-backed transfer web, a strip of hook and loop tape 3" (7.5 cm) long.

• **INSTRUCTIONS**

Make a full-size paper pattern of the applique motifs. Trace the complete pattern 3 times onto the transfer web. Cut the traced motifs apart in sections, according to their color (use the photo as a guide). Fuse them to the corresponding fabric: treetops in green, doors in dark green, roofs in red, buildings in white, and the streams in blue. The bridge, the tree trunks, and the windows are not appliqued but are sewn in satin stitch. Cut all motifs along the tracing lines.

With right sides together and 1/4" (1 cm) seam allowance, sew the blue and green strips together along one long edge. Use the paper pattern as a guide for positioning the motifs.

Remove the backing from the motifs and press them onto the strip, centering the first pattern and repeating once at each side. Stitch the motifs with matching thread and with an open, narrow zigzag stitch. Trace the windows, tree trunks, and bridge onto the fabric. Stitch them in satin stitch—a very close zigzag stitch—with an appropriate stitch width.

Fold the piece in half lengthwise, with right sides together. Stitch around the raw edges, leaving an opening at the center of the long edge for turning. Clip corners and turn right side out. Attach the hook and loop tape to the ends to fasten the tieback around the curtain. ■

118

Stencil Pattern for Curtain Tieback. Shown 75% of actual size; photocopy at 133%.

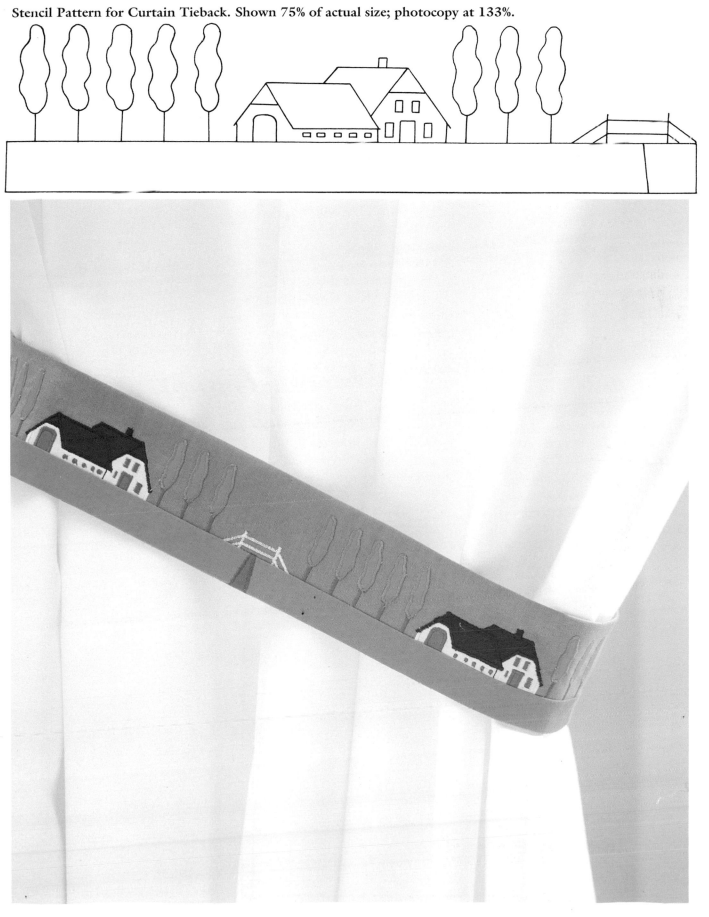

LOG CABIN COMFORTER COVER

〜

• FINISHED MEASUREMENTS

79" (197 cm) square.

• MATERIALS

Cotton fabric in 4 different complementary prints, 2 light colored and 2 dark colored, and one coordinating solid dark color. Cotton fabric for backing and flap, 4-7/8 yds (4.5 m) at 45" (115 cm) wide or 4-1/2 yds (4 m) at 54–56" (140 cm) wide. Thread.

• INSTRUCTIONS

Using the photo as a guide for color arrangement, cut pieces 2, 3, 6, and 7 from lighter fabric, and pieces 4, 5, 8, and 9 from darker fabric. For piece 1, cut a piece 27" (68 cm) square from the solid color. Cut piece 2, 14" x 27" (35 cm x 68 cm). Cut pieces 3 and 4, 14" x 40-1/4" (35 cm x 101 cm). Cut pieces 5 and 6, 14" x 53-1/2" (35 cm x 134 cm). Cut

pieces 7 and 8, 14" x 66-3/4" (35 cm x 167 cm). Cut piece 9, 14" x 80" (35 cm x 200 cm).

Sew the strips with right sides together and with exactly 3/8" (1 cm) seams, using the sketch as a guide for placement. First sew strip 2 to the center square. Then sew on strip 3, 4, 5, and so on.

For the backing, cut 2 pieces 40-1/2" x 78" (101 cm x 195 cm). For the flap, cut 2 pieces 7" x 40-1/4" (18 cm x 101 cm). With right sides together and 1/4" (1 cm) seam allowance, sew the backing pieces together along one narrow end and sew the flap pieces together along one narrow edge. Clip selvages and press seams open. Hem one long edge of the flap and one narrow edge of the backing with 1" (3 cm) double hems.

Place the pieced front right side up, and place the flap on top, right side down, with raw edges together along the upper edge of the cover. Place the backing on top of these pieces, right side down, with raw edges even along the lower edge of the cover. Stitch around all 4 sides with 1/2" (1.5 cm) seam allowance. Trim corners and turn right side out. ∎

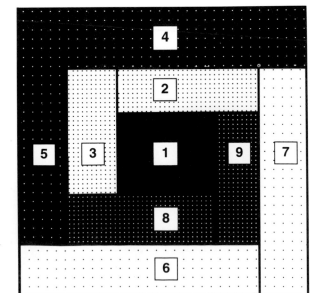

Pattern for Log Cabin Comforter Cover

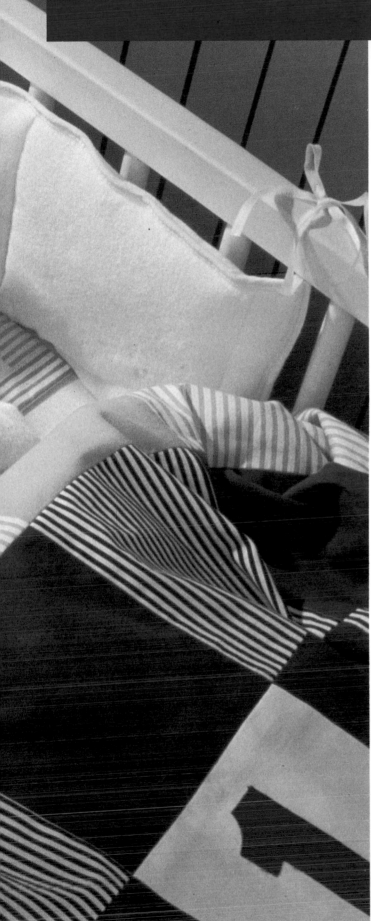

PATCHWORK BLANKET & PILLOW

.... ℘ ....

N o room in the house is more fun to fix up than the nursery. There's something about working on a small scale, and for a small person, that encourages creativity and playfulness. A patchwork blanket and pillowcase in primary colors will brighten up an already happy room.

**Pattern for Baby
Blanket & Pillow**

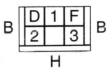

A	B	A	B	A	B	A
B	C	D	C	D	C	B
A	D	C	1	C	D	A
B	C	2		3	C	B
A	F	E	F	E	F	A
B	G	H	G	H	G	B
A	H	G	H	G	H	A
B	A	B	A	B	A	B

Patchwork Crib Blanket Cover and Pillowcase

§

• **Finished Measurements**

Blanket cover 45" x 51-1/2" (117 cm x 134 cm). Pillowcase 17-1/2" x 24" (46 cm x 63 cm).

• **Materials**

BLANKET

For the front, 56 pieces of cotton fabric 7" (18 cm) square in the following colors: 13 yellow, 13 yellow striped, 7 blue, 4 blue striped, 5 green, 5 green striped, 2 red, 3 red striped, 4 white. For the backing, yellow cotton fabric 46" x 51-1/2" (120 cm x 134 cm). For the backing flap, yellow cotton 8" x 45" (20 cm x 120 cm). 5 buttons, 3/4" (2 cm) diameter.

PILLOWCASE

For the front, 6 pieces of cotton 7" (18 cm) square: 4 white, 1 blue striped, 1 red striped. Yellow striped fabric, 2 pieces 3" x 13-1/2" (8 cm x 35 cm). Green striped fabric, 2 pieces 3" x 25" (8 cm x 56 cm). For the pillowcase backing, yellow cotton 18-1/2" x 24" (49 cm x 63 cm). Fusible web, white and red thread.

• **Instructions**

APPLIQUES

Trace the numerals and cut 2 of each from the red fabric. Center them on white squares and press in place with fusible web. Stitch around the numerals with a straight stitch, about 1/8" (.2 cm) from the edges. Using a close zigzag stitch, sew around all edges, covering the raw edge of the numeral and the line of straight stitching.

BLANKET COVER FRONT

Use 1/4" (.5 cm) seam allowance except where otherwise noted. Following the chart, sew the squares together in strips. Press seams open. Sew the strips together; press.

BACKING AND FLAP

Hem one short end of the backing with a 1" (3 cm) double hem. Hem one long edge of the backing flap in the same way. Make 5 buttonholes across the hemmed edge of the flap and perpendicular to it, about 3/4" (2 cm) from the edge. Place the outer buttonholes 2" (5 cm) from the ends of the flap and space the others evenly across the flap.

ASSEMBLY

Place the pieced front right side up, and place the flap on top, right side down, with raw edges even along upper edge of the cover. Place the backing on top of these pieces, right side down, with raw edges even along the lower edge of the cover. Stitch around all 4 sides with 1/2" (1.5 cm) seam allowance. Trim corners and turn right side out. Sew on buttons, using buttonholes to mark position.

PILLOWCASE

For the front, piece the squares in strips and assemble as for the blanket cover. Sew a yellow striped piece to each short end of the pieced front. Sew a green striped piece to each long side. Hem one long edge of the backing flap and one short end of the backing with 1" (3 cm) double hems. Assemble the front, backing, and flap as for the blanket cover. ■

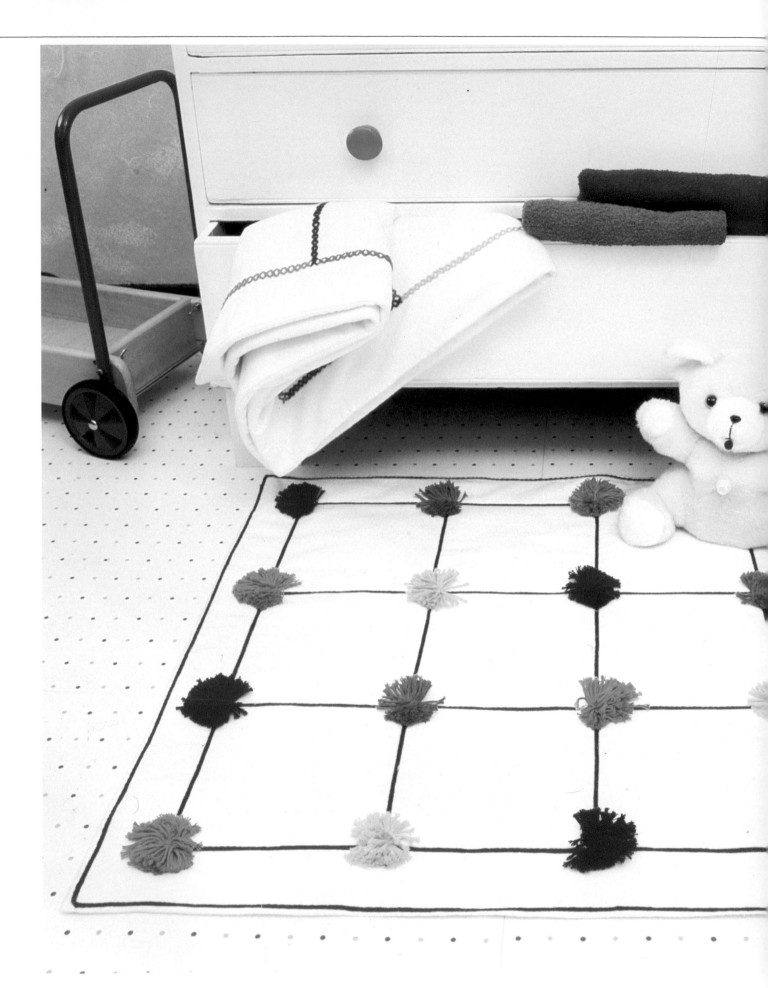

NURSERY IN PRIMARY COLORS

············ ❦ ············

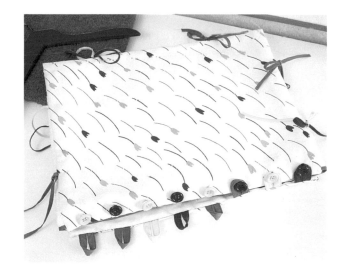

A rug with bright pompons will warm the feet of any parent walking the floor in the middle of the night. The same pattern can be used instead to make a cheerful crib blanket.

And to help keep track of an infant's endless paraphernalia, there's a "baby organizer" made from fabric, with pockets for everything. It folds up neatly for storage or travel (as shown in the photo above) or hangs conveniently close to the crib (see page 128).

Baby Rug or Blanket

~

● **Finished Measurements**

30" x 38" (75 cm x 95 cm).

● **Materials**

White cotton flannel 32" x 40"
(80 cm x 100 cm), washable felt
or a second piece of flannel 32" x 40"
(80 cm x 100 cm), worsted weight
cotton yarn in yellow, green, red,
and turquoise. Felt-tip fabric
marking pen, thread.

● **Instructions**

Position the felt and flannel with
right sides together and stitch a 1"
(2.5 cm) seam around all edges,
leaving an opening on 1 side for
turning. Trim corners and turn
right side out. Stitch across opening. Mark the grid pattern on the
flannel side. Sew 3 strands of red
yarn along the lines with a zigzag
stitch.

To make pompons, cut strands of
yarn 2-3/4" (7 cm) long. Tie the
strands together tightly in the
center and sew them at the inter-
sections in the grid as shown in the
photo. ■

Baby Organizer

~

● **Finished Measurements**

16" x 48" (40 cm x 120 cm) open, 16"
x 12" (40 cm x 30 cm) closed.

● **Materials**

2 yds (1.8 m) heavy white cotton
fabric 45" (115 cm) wide, floral print
fabric 18" x 50" (45 cm x 125 cm),
white terrycloth 20-1/2" x 10-1/2"
(51 cm x 26 cm), white washable felt
or cotton flannel 18" x 50" (45 cm x
125 cm). 4 red and 4 yellow buttons,
3/4" (2 cm) diameter, double fold
bias seam binding 3/4" (2 cm) wide,
1 package each of red, yellow, green,
and aqua. Elastic 1/8" (.5 cm) wide,
1/2 yd (46 cm), thread, dowel rod
1/2" (2 cm) diameter, 20" (51 cm)
long.

● **Instructions**

Make paper patterns for the pockets
according to the measurements on
the diagram. For pockets 1, 2, 6, 7,
and 8, add 2" (6 cm) on each side for
pleats and seam allowance. Cut 1 of
each from white cotton fabric. For
pockets 3, 4, and 5, cut 1 of each by

the pattern, with no added seam
allowance.

For pockets 1, 2, 6, 7, and 8, turn
under 1/2" (1 cm) at each side and
press. Make a 3/8" (1 cm) pleat on
each side at the bottom edge. On the
outside, fold the pleat even with the
pressed edge of the pocket. Press the
pleats flat. Bind the vertical crease of
each pleat with bias tape, varying the
colors as shown in the photograph.
Baste pleats across lower edge. Bind
the lower edge with bias tape,
turning under the ends of the tape at
the sides of the pocket. Bind the
upper edge in the same way.

On pockets 3, 4, and 5, bind all 4
edges with bias tape. Use a different
color of tape for each edge, and fold
under the overlapping end of the
tape.

To make the pocket backing, sew the
felt to the wrong side of the large
piece of white cotton with 1/4"

(1 cm) seam allowance. On the front (the cotton side) mark placement lines for pockets 1 through 8, following the diagram. Mark the 3 foldlines.

Position pockets 1, 2, 6, 7, and 8 on the backing. Sew the sides to the backing through all thicknesses up 1" (3 cm) from the bottom, then sew only the pressed edges to the backing from there to the top, keeping the pleat free. Backstitch the ends of all seams for security.

Position pockets 4 and 5 on the backing, easing the top and bottom slightly to create a pouch. Sew top and bottom to the backing, leaving sides open.

Sew the sides and bottom of pocket 3 to the backing. Sew 5 vertical lines of stitching to subdivide the pocket.

For pocket 9, the lower double pocket, cut a piece of white cotton 15-1/2" x 10-1/2" (37 cm x 26 cm). With the right side of the cotton to the wrong side of the terrycloth, sew the sides together with 1/4" (1 cm) seam allowance. Bind the seams with tape. Fold a pleat at the bottom of the terrycloth on each side so that the lower edge of the terrycloth is the same length as the lower edge of the cotton. Baste the pleats in place and bind the lower edges together with bias tape, folding under the ends at the side seams. Bind all around the top edge. Position the pocket on the backing *upside down*, with the terrycloth side out. Place the sides of the pocket 1-1/2" (4 cm) from the edges of the backing, the top of the pocket 1-1/2" (4 cm) above the bottom edge of the backing, and the bottom of the pocket on the lower foldline. Sew across the lower edge of the pocket. Sew the sides to the backing as for the other pleated pockets.

For the button loops/hangers, cut 8 strips of bias tape in different colors, each 4" (10 cm) long. Mark placement points for the loops along the top edge of the backing piece, on the right side. Mark the first 2 points 2" (5 cm) in from the sides, and the other 6 spaced at 2" (5 cm) intervals across the top. Fold the bias strips in half. Place the ends even with the top edge, centered over the mark, and the loop toward the inside. Pin in place.

For the ties, cut 12 pieces of bias tape 12" (30 cm) long. On 8 strips, turn under 1 end and stitch, then stitch the long folded edges together. On the other 4, finish both ends and stitch the long folded edges together. Position the first 8 ties on the backing, 3-1/4" and 8-3/4" (8 cm and 22 cm) down from the top on each side, and 3 1/4" and 8-3/4" (8 cm and 22 cm) up from the bottom on each side. Pin them in place, with the unfinished end even with the edge of the backing and the finished end to the inside.

Pin the floral fabric to the pocket backing with right sides together. Stitch around the edges, taking care not to catch ties and pocket edges in the seam. Leave about 10" (25 cm) open at the center of one long side for turning. Clip corners and turn right side out. Stitch across the opening. Stitch across the piece along the 3 marked foldlines.

Sew the 4 remaining bias ties to the back of the piece. Place 2 on the upper foldline and 2 on the lower foldline, 4" (10 cm) in from the sides. Sew one end of each tie securely at the foldline.

Cut 8 strips of elastic 3" (8 cm) long. Spacing them the same as the button loops at the top of the piece, pin them to the front side of the piece with the ends together 1/2" (1 cm) above the center foldline and the loops downward. Cut a strip of bias tape 17" (42 cm) long. Open out

the center fold and press flat. Turn under 1/2" (1 cm) at each end and press. Center the strip over the lower foldline, covering the ends of the elastic loops. Stitch it in place along both edges.

Sew buttons to the back of the piece, 1" (3 cm) above the lower edge. Space them to correspond to the loops at the top of the piece and the elastic loops at the center.

To hang the organizer, slip upper loops over the dowel, fold the lower section up and button with the elastic loops. To use the organizer as a carryall, fold at the upper foldline and button at the center with the upper loops. ∎

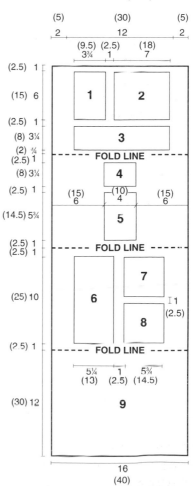

Inches (CM)

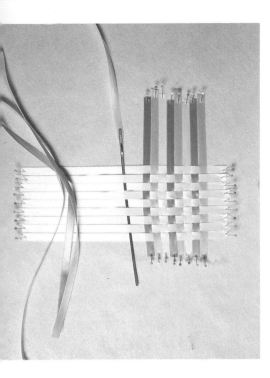

white ribbon to the cardboard as shown in the photo. With the weaving needle, weave in the colored ribbons, alternating colors. Pin the ends of the ribbons in place so they are even around the outer edges. Using a pressing cloth, steam press the ribbons to fuse them lightly to the interfacing. Let dry and carefully remove the piece from the cardboard. With the piece upside down, fuse according to the instructions with the interfacing.

Place the woven piece and the cotton with right sides together. Sewing on the ribbon side, stitch around the edges close to the weaving with about 1/4" (1 cm) seam allowance. Leave an opening on one edge for turning. Clip corners and turn right side out. Stuff with fiberfill and stitch across opening. ∎

Woven Pincushion

∽

• **FINISHED MEASUREMENTS**
5-7/8" x 7-3/8" (16 cm x 20 cm).

• **MATERIALS**
Polyester satin ribbon 3/8" (1 cm) wide: 4 yds (3.7 m) white, 1-3/4 yds (1.5 m) pink, 1-3/8 yds (1.3 m) each of green and yellow. Weaving needle, white cotton fabric 6-1/2" x 8" (18 cm x 22 cm), loose-pack fiberfill, lightweight fusible interfacing 10" x 12" (26 cm x 30 cm), corrugated cardboard.

• **INSTRUCTIONS**
Cut 15 strips of white ribbon 9-1/2" (24 cm) long. Cut 6 strips of yellow and green and 7 strips of pink ribbon 8" (20 cm) long. Cut a piece of corrugated cardboard the size of the interfacing and place the interfacing on it, glue side up. Pin the lengths of

Woven Crib Quilt

∽

• **FINISHED MEASUREMENTS**
40" x 30" (100 cm x 75 cm).

• **MATERIALS**
2-3/8 yds (2.1 m) white cotton fabric 45" (115 cm) wide, 1 yd (.8 m) each pink, green, and yellow cotton fabric 45" (115 cm) wide, 1-3/4 yds (1.6 m) fiberfill batting, medium thickness, 72" (180 cm) wide.

• **INSTRUCTIONS**
For the border, cut 2 strips of white cotton 31" x 4-3/4" (78 cm x 12 cm) and 2 strips 40-3/4" x 4-3/4" (102 cm x 12 cm). Cut 2 strips of batting 40-3/4" x 2-1/2" (102 cm x 6 cm) and 2 strips 31" x 2-1/2" (78 cm x 6 cm). For the bands for weaving, cut 10

white strips and 5 strips of batting 40" x 6" (100 cm x 15 cm). Cut strips 30" x 6" (75 cm x 15 cm): 6 pink, 4 green, 4 yellow, and 7 from batting.

For weaving, make 5 white, 3 pink, 2 yellow, and 2 green bands. To make a band, place 2 strips of the same color with right sides together and pin a strip of batting on top. Stitch the long edges with 1/4" (1 cm) seam allowance. Trim batting close to the stitching, turn right side out, and press.

Place the 5 white bands side by side, lengthwise, on a table and weave the colored bands through them, alternating colors as shown in the photo. Have all ends extending evenly on the edges. Stitch around the outer edges, stitching only through the unfinished ends. Trim the ends to 1/2" (1.5 cm). Trim batting close to the stitching in the ends of the bands.

Press the border strips in half, lengthwise, right side out. Place a batting strip on the border, with raw edges even. Sew the border strips and batting to the edges with right sides together and 1/4" (1 cm) seam allowance. Begin and end stitching 1/4" (1 cm) from the ends of the border strips, and stitch only through the unfinished ends of the bands, keeping the long edges of the interwoven strips free. Miter the corners: at each corner, stitch border strips together from the ends of the previous stitching lines to the lengthwise crease at a 45-degree angle, so that the corner will lie flat. Trim batting to stitching. Fold border to the inside along the crease. Turn under the raw edge to just cover the previous stitching line; press. Miter the inner corners by folding at a 45-degree angle to match outer corners. Trim off excess fabric; press; stitch. Stitch around inner edge of border close to fold. ∎

THROW PILLOWS

·········· ✍ ··········

Groupings of throw pillows add charm and individuality to a room. By varying the colors and fabrics, you can get quite different effects from the same pillow pattern. We've done the same pillows in pink and green (shown here), in red (page 140), and in beige (page 144). For good measure, we've given each room a couple that are unique.

Stencil for Painted Pillow with Flowered Border. Shown at 100%.

PILLOW WITH BOW

∾

- **FINISHED MEASUREMENTS**

20" (50 cm) square.

- **MATERIALS**

5/8 yd (.6 m) green/white striped fabric 45" (115 cm) wide, pink cotton fabric 19" (49 cm) square, small piece of flowered chintz, pink thread, kraft paper, tracing paper, glue stick. For the inner pillow, 3/4 yd (.6 m) white cotton fabric 45" (115 cm) wide, loose-pack fiberfill.

- **INSTRUCTIONS**

Make a full-size copy of the motif. Trace the bow onto pink fabric and cut along the tracing lines. Cut a piece of paper 18-1/2" (46 cm) square. Trace the one corner shape on all 4 corners of the paper. Cut the pattern on the traced lines. Use this pattern to cut the front and back from green striped fabric, adding 1/2" (1.5 cm) seam allowance. Cut the small pieces of the motif from flowered fabric.

Position the motif pieces on the pillow front with glue stick. Stitch around all edges with a zigzag stitch, overcasting the edges at the same time.

Sew the front to the back with right sides together, leaving 12" (30 cm) open on one side. Trim the corners and turn right side out.

Use the paper pattern to cut the lining front and back from the white cotton, adding 1/2" (1.5 cm) seam allowance. Sew the back to the front with right sides together, leaving an opening on one side. Trim and turn right side out. Stuff the lining with fiberfill and stitch the opening. Put the inner pillow into the cover, and stitch across the opening. ∎

PAINTED PILLOW WITH FLOWERS

∾

- **FINISHED MEASUREMENTS**

20-3/4" (22 cm) square.

- **MATERIALS**

1-1/2 yds (1.2 m) red flowered chintz, 5/8 yd (.5 m) hardanger cloth (red/white) 60" (150 cm) wide, 1-1/4" yds (1 m) beige seam binding 1/2" (1.5 cm) wide, light green, dark green, red, and pink fabric paints, 2 stenciling brushes, dressmakers' carbon, stenciling acetate, craft knife, pillow form

- **INSTRUCTIONS**

Cut 4 strips of flowered chintz

2-3/4" x 21-3/4" (7 cm x 54.5 cm) for the outer border. For the back, cut 2 pieces 11-3/4" x 22" (29.5 cm x 55 cm). Cut a 20" (50 cm) square from hardanger cloth, placing the large border and seam allowance at the outer edges of the square.

Make a full-size copy of the motif and trace it onto the acetate. Cut out the design areas. Position the motif 1/4" (1 cm) inside the double red stripes, with a red flower at each corner. Paint the flowers red and the leaves and stems dark green. Reposition the stencil for each corner, using the photo as a guide. Turn the stencil to paint motifs between the corners. Use pink for the center flowers, and light green for their stems and leaves. Trim the edges of the square to 1/2" (1.5 cm) outside the double lines. Finish the front and back as for the cross stitch pillow, omitting the ribbons. ∎

Pattern for Pillow
with Bow. Shown
50% of actual size;
photocopy at 200%.

ROUND RUFFLED PILLOW

• **FINISHED MEASUREMENTS**
20-3/4" (52 cm) in diameter.

• **MATERIALS**
5/8 yd (.5 m) flowered cotton chintz 45" (115 cm) wide, 1/2 yd (.4 m) red/white striped chintz 45" (115 cm) wide, 16 covered button forms 3/4" (2 cm) in diameter. Kraft paper, compass, sewing thread, heavy thread, pillow form.

• **INSTRUCTIONS**
On paper, draw a circle 16" (40 cm) in diameter, and add 1/4" (1 cm) seam allowance. Use this pattern to cut 2 circles from flowered chintz. Cut 2 strips 5-1/2" x 48" (14 cm x 120 cm) from the striped chintz. Sew the pieces with right sides together and with 1/4" (1 cm) seam allowance. Sew the strips together at both ends to form a ring. Fold in half, right side out. Stitch the raw edges together with 2 rows of machine basting, 1/8" and 3/8" (.5 cm and 1.5 cm) from the edge. Gather the ruffle to fit the circle. Stitch the gathers in place, inside the seamline. Sew the ruffle to a circle.

Sew the back to the front, leaving 10" (25 cm) open. Trim the seam allowance and turn right side out. Insert the pillow form and stitch across the opening. Cover the buttons with striped fabric. Sew on the buttons through the pillow with heavy thread, attaching each button on the front to one on the back. ∎

PILLOW WITH TIED CORNERS

• **FINISHED MEASUREMENTS**
20-3/4" (52 cm) square.

• **MATERIALS**
3/4 yd (.6 m) blue/white striped cotton fabric 45" (115 cm) wide, 1 yd (.9 m) floral print cotton fabric 45" (15 cm) wide, 9-1/2 yds (8.5 m) green double fold bias tape 1/2" (1.5 cm) wide, white and green thread, 1-1/4 yds (1 m) beige double fold bias tape 1/2" (1.5 cm) wide. Tracing paper, pillow form.

• **INSTRUCTIONS**
Make a full-size copy of the pattern for the tie ends. From the flowered fabric, cut 8 strips 4" x 40" (10 cm x 100 cm). Fold the strips in half, lengthwise. Use the pattern to cut the ends, placing the dotted line of the pattern on the fold of the fabric.

Cut a 21-1/2" (54 cm) square from the striped fabric, centering the stripes. Cut 2 striped pieces 11-1/2" x 21-1/2" (29 cm x 54 cm) for the back.

Bind the edges of the flowered strips: sew the bias tape to the wrong side, with raw edges even, and fold it over the edge to the right side. Stitch close to the edge of the tape. Sew the strips to the pillow front piece, with the outer edges of the strips 3/8" (1.5 cm) inside the edges of the front. Begin and end stitching 4-3/4" (12 cm) from the corners so ends are free. Assemble and finish the pillow as for the cross stitch pillow. ∎

BOUQUET PILLOW

• **FINISHED MEASUREMENTS**
16" x 18" (40 cm x 45 cm).

• **MATERIALS**
3/4 yd (.6 m) beige cotton fabric 45" (115 cm) wide, small pieces of light green, green, white, pink, flowered, narrow blue/white striped, and wide blue/white striped cotton fabrics. Tracing paper, glue stick, dressmakers' carbon, fusible interfacing, pink, blue, and green thread, loose-pack fiberfill.

• **INSTRUCTIONS**
Make a full-size copy of the motif. For the back and front, cut the entire pattern from doubled beige fabric, adding 1/2" (1.5 cm) seam allowance around all edges. Fuse interfacing to the wrong side of the small fabric pieces. Trace the individual motifs onto the fabrics, using the photo as a guide for color. Cut out all the separate pieces, and arrange them on the cushion front piece, keeping within the 1/2" (1.5 cm) seam allowance. Secure them in place with glue stick. Applique the pieces with matching thread. Use a zigzag stitch, overcasting the raw edges.

Place the front and back with right sides together and stitch around all edges, leaving 6" (15 cm) open at the lower edge. Trim seams and turn right side out. Stuff with fiberfill and stitch across the opening. ∎

Bouquet Pillow Pattern.
Shown 50% of actual
size; photocopy at 200%.

PILLOW WITH CROSS STITCH CENTER

∽

• FINISHED MEASUREMENTS
22" (55 cm) square.

• MATERIALS
Flemish linen 14" (35 cm) square with 26 threads per inch, embroidery floss in colors indicated, 1/4 yd (.2 m) floral print chintz 45" (115 cm) wide, 3/8 yd (.25 m) green/white striped chintz 45" (115 cm) wide, 3/4 yd (.7 m) red/white striped chintz 45" (115 cm) wide, 4 yds (3.6 m) pink ribbon 1/2" (1.5 cm) wide, thread, 1-1/8 yd (1 m) beige double fold bias tape 1/2" (1.5 cm) wide, pillow form.

• INSTRUCTIONS
Cut the striped fabrics with the stripes centered on each piece. For the front, cut 4 pieces from the floral print 3-1/4" x 15-1/2" (8 cm x 39 cm). Cut from the green/white striped fabric 4 strips 4" x 22" (10 cm x 55 cm). Cut from the red/white striped fabric 4 strips 1-1/4" x 23" (3.5 cm x 58 cm), cutting them from the red stripe. For the back, cut from the red/white striped fabric 2 pieces 12-1/4" x 23" (31 cm x 58 cm).

Mark a 10" (25 cm) square on the linen with a basting stitch. Mark the center of the linen square and of the graph as a guide for stitching. Work the floral design in cross stitch, using 3 strands of floss over 3 threads. Cut the embroidery 1/4" (1 cm) outside the basting lines.

Sew all pieces with right sides together and with 1/4" (1 cm) seam allowances. Sew a floral strip, a green striped strip, and a red striped strip together, using the photo as a guide. Make a total of 4 pieced strips. Sew strips together diagonally at the corners (at a 45-degree angle), beginning the seam at the outer edge. Trim seams. Cut the ribbon into 4 equal lengths. Center each over the seam between the striped and the floral strips. Sew ribbon to 1/8" (.5 cm) from the corner seams. Tie a bow at each corner. Sew the center square in place.

Sew the 2 back pieces together along one long edge with a 3/4" (2 cm) seam, leaving the center 16" (40 cm) open. Press the seam open. Fold under the seam allowances of the opening, and stitch. Cut the seam binding into 4 equal pieces and sew 2 to each side of the opening. Place the back and front pieces together and stitch around the edges. Trim the corners and turn right side out. Insert the pillow form. ■

Pink Color Key

		DMC	Anchor
◣	Dark Pink	309	39
◢	Dark Green	561	218
◹	Light Green	564	206
𝗜	Salmon Pink	754	4146
•	Light Pink	776	49
✚	Pink	899	31
◸	Green	912	209

Red Color Key

		DMC	Anchor
◣	Dark Red	498	44
◢	Dark Green	561	212
◹	Light Green	563	203
𝗜	Yellow	742	302
•	Pink	957	52
✚	Dark Pink	603	62
◸	Green	911	230

Beige Color Key

All cross-stitch areas

	DMC	Anchor
Light Brown	613	831

RED
PILLOWS

············ ✿ ············

This grouping
of pillows fairly
shouts—red! Most
of these pillows appear in
different colors on page 132;
use the patterns that follow
that page to make your
scarlet versions. But we've
added a pillow with bright
pompons (for a little extra
color) and a casual-looking
tied pillow, as well.

POMPON PILLOW

• FINISHED MEASUREMENTS
20" x 20" (50 cm x 50 cm)

• MATERIALS
3/4 yd (.55 m) striped fabric 60" (150 cm) wide, 16" x 16" (40 cm x 40 cm) red fabric, colorful cotton yarn (pink, yellow, green and black), pillow form.

• INSTRUCTIONS
Cut a piece of red cotton fabric 15" square (38 cm x 38 cm), for the center of the front. Cut a piece of striped fabric 20-3/4" square (52 cm x 52 cm) for the back. Cut 4 strips of striped fabric 3-1/2" x 20-3/4" (9 cm x 52 cm), to make the front border.

Sew the long strips together end to end, right sides together, with 45 degree mitered corners. With right sides together, sew the red cotton square to the striped border. Press the seams open. Place the back and front right sides together, and stitch around the outside, leaving a 16" (40 cm) opening on one side. Turn right side out, insert the pillow form, and hand sew the opening closed.

Make 8 pompons from the cotton yarn. Cut 2 cardboard circles 3" (8

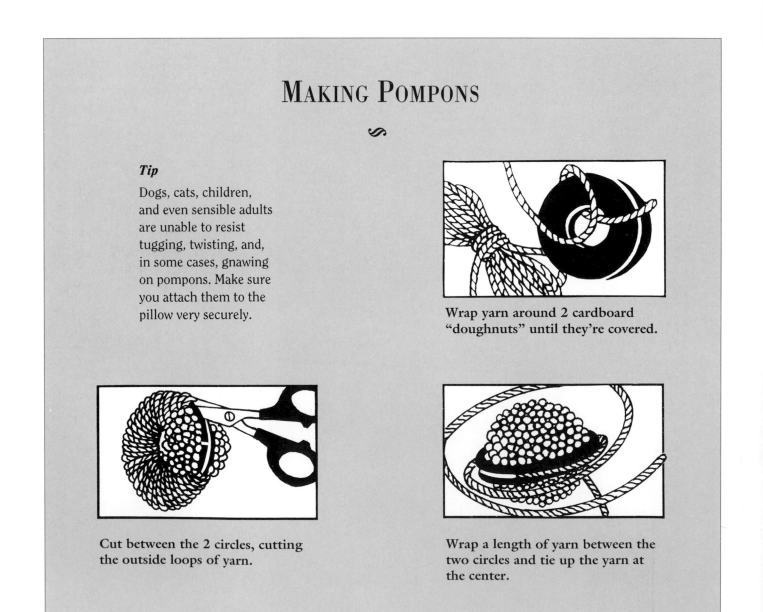

MAKING POMPONS

Tip

Dogs, cats, children, and even sensible adults are unable to resist tugging, twisting, and, in some cases, gnawing on pompons. Make sure you attach them to the pillow very securely.

Wrap yarn around 2 cardboard "doughnuts" until they're covered.

Cut between the 2 circles, cutting the outside loops of yarn.

Wrap a length of yarn between the two circles and tie up the yarn at the center.

cm) in diameter. Cut a 1" (3 cm) circle in the center, so that you have 2 doughnut-shaped pieces of cardboard. Place the 2 circles together, then wrap the yarn around and around the form in the same direction, as shown in the drawings, until it is covered evenly and completely. Cut a 6" (15 cm) length of matching yarn for the binding. Cut between the two circles, so that you cut through the outside loops of yarn. Slip the 6" (15 cm) length of yarn between the cardboard circles, and wrap it tightly around all the yarn where it passes through the center of the pattern. Tie tightly. Trim the yarn ends to a good pompon shape, and hand sew the pompons to the pillow, spacing them about 2" (5 cm) apart. ■

TIED PILLOW

~

• **FINISHED MEASUREMENTS**
About 16" x 20" (40 cm x 50 cm)

• **MATERIALS**
Printed fabric 44" x 44" (110 cm x

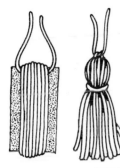

To make tassels, wrap cardboard with yarn, tie, and trim.

110 cm), 5 yds (4.5 m) red bias seam binding, red thread, small amount of red yarn, a piece of cardboard, pillow form 16" x 20" (40 cm x 50 cm).

• **INSTRUCTIONS**
Sew the bias seam binding along edges of fabric. Make 2 tassels from red yarn: cut 2 pieces of cardboard 2-3/4" (7 cm) long and wrap yarn around cardboard as shown in sketch. Thread a piece of yarn through the top loop and another piece around the tassel. Cut and trim the bottom ends. Sew a tassel on each of 2 opposite corners. Place the pillow form in the center of the fabric and wrap the fabric over the form. Sew the ends without tassels together, and tie the tasseled ends together. ■

PILLOW WITH RED BOW

~

• **FINISHED MEASUREMENTS**
20" (50 cm) square.

• **MATERIALS**
3/4 yd (.6 m) red flowered fabric 45" (115 cm) wide, red cotton fabric 19" (49 cm) square, a small piece of pink cotton, red thread, 1-1/4 yds (1 m) red double fold bias tape 1/2" (1.5 cm) wide. Kraft paper, tracing paper, glue stick. For the inner pillow, 3/4 yd (.6 m) white cotton fabric 45" (115 cm) wide, loose-pack fiberfill.

• **INSTRUCTIONS**
Make this pillow following the

directions for the pillow with the pink bow, but use flowered fabric for the pillow front and back, and red and pink fabrics for the bow and ribbon. Applique in zigzag stitch with red thread. ■

PILLOW WITH RED BOUQUET

~

• **FINISHED MEASUREMENTS**
16" x 18" (40 cm x 45 cm).

• **MATERIALS**
3/4 yd (.6 m) dark red cotton fabric 45" (115 cm) wide, small pieces of green, dark green, pink, black, and red fabric, and 2 different printed cotton fabrics. Tracing paper, dressmakers' carbon, glue stick, fusible interfacing, red and black thread, loose-pack fiberfill.

• **INSTRUCTIONS**
Follow the directions for making the pink and blue bouquet pillow. Cut the flower pot from dark red fabric. Cut center leaves from green fabric, outer leaves from dark green, flower centers from black, and flowers from the prints, using the photo as a guide. Applique the pieces to the background with black thread. Stitch the lines around the flower centers with a very narrow zigzag stitch, and the lines on the pot with a zigzag stitch 1/2" (.5 cm) wide. ■

LINEN PILLOW WITH BOW

❧

• **FINISHED MEASUREMENTS**

20" (50 cm) square.

• **MATERIALS**

3/4 yd (.6 m) natural linen 45" (115 cm) wide, white cotton fabric 19" (49 cm) square, small piece of light brown printed cotton fabric, light brown thread, 1-1/4 yds (1 m) beige double fold bias tape 1/2" (1.5 cm) wide. Kraft paper, tracing paper, glue stick. For the inner pillow, 3/4 yd (.6 m) white cotton fabric 45" (115 cm) wide, loose-pack fiberfill.

• **INSTRUCTIONS**

Make this pillow following the directions for the pillow with the pink bow, but use linen for the pillow front and back. Cut the ribbon and bow from white cotton, and the inside of the bow from printed fabric. Applique in zigzag stitch with light brown thread. ■

FOLDED PILLOW WITH BOWS

❧

• **FINISHED MEASUREMENTS**

20" x 20" (50 cm x 50 cm)

• **MATERIALS**

3/4 yd (.55 m) white fabric 56" (140 cm) wide, 1 yd (.75 m) ecru linen 56" (140 cm) wide, 4-1/2 yds (4 m) ecru seam binding 1/2" (1.5 cm) wide, pillow form.

• **INSTRUCTIONS**

Cut 2 squares of white fabric 20-3/4" x 20-3/4" (52 cm x 52 cm) for back. Cut a square from linen 28-3/4" x 28-3/4" (72 cm x 72 cm). Cut out 18 pieces of seam binding 8-3/4" (22 cm) long. Place the 2 pieces of white fabric right sides together and sew them together on 3 sides with a 1/4" (1 cm) seam allowance. Leave a 16" (40 cm) opening on the fourth side. Turn right side out, insert pillow form, and sew opening closed. Hem all 4 edges of the ecru linen with a 1/4" (1 cm) hem. Turn the edges under and hem 1/4" (1 cm) again, creating a hem with an inner hem. Place the pillow on the wrong side of fabric with the corners at the center of each side of pillow. Fold the corners over the top of the pillow. At 4-1/4" and 8-3/4" (11 and 22 cm) from each corner, sew on a piece of seam binding to each side of linen square as shown on photo. Tie bows. Sew a piece of seam binding to 2 opposite corners so as to tie ends in a bow at center of pillow. ∎

PILLOW WITH WHITE BOUQUET

• FINISHED MEASUREMENTS
16" x 18" (40 cm x 45 cm).

• MATERIALS
3/4 yd (.6 m) beige cotton fabric 45" (115 cm) wide, small pieces of green/white striped fabric and of unbleached cotton muslin, white cotton fabric 14" x 18" (35 cm x 45 cm), small pieces of light brown polka dot fabric, tracing paper, glue stick, fusible interfacing, ecru thread, loose-pack fiberfill

• INSTRUCTIONS
Make this pillow according to the directions for the pink and blue bouquet pillow, but cut the flowers as a single piece from white fabric and the leaves as a single piece from muslin. Cut the flower pot from striped fabric and the flower centers from muslin. Trace the outlines of the flowers and leaves onto the fabric and sew over them with a moderately wide zigzag stitch, using ecru thread. ∎

PATCHWORK PILLOW

• FINISHED MEASUREMENTS
24" (61 cm) square.

• MATERIALS
10 different printed and solid-colored pieces of cotton fabric, white cotton fabric 10" x 26" (25 cm x 65 cm), 3/8 yd (.25 m) pink cotton fabric with a white print 45" (115 cm) wide, flowered chintz 6" x 20" (15 cm x 50 cm), 3/4 yd (.7 m) red/white striped chintz, 1-1/4 yds (1 m) beige double fold bias tape 1/2" (1.5 cm) wide, pillow form, kraft paper, cardboard, craft knife, rotary cutter and mat or sharp scissors.

• INSTRUCTIONS
From the flowered chintz, cut 4 pieces 4-3/4" (12 cm) square. Cut 4 strips of pink cotton 4-3/4" x 16-1/4" (12 cm x 41 cm). From striped chintz, cut 4 red strips 1-1/4" x 25-1/2" (3.5 cm x 64 cm). For the back, cut 2 pieces 13-1/2" x 25-1/2" (34 cm x 64 cm) from red/white striped fabric.

For the patchwork, make a paper pattern 1-1/4" (3 cm) square. Cut 2 paper squares 3-1/2" (9 cm) on a side. Cut one large square in half diagonally to make 2 triangles. Cut 1 triangle in half to make 2 small triangles of equal size. Add precisely 1/8" (.5 cm) seam allowance around all edges of the paper patterns and cut cardboard templates from them.

Cut 81 small triangles from the printed fabrics. Cut 4 large squares, 8 large triangles, and 4 small triangles from white cotton. Sew all pieces with right sides together and with *exactly* 1/8" (.5 cm) seam allowance.

Make bands of 3 small printed squares. Sew 3 bands together to make a 4" (10 cm) square. Make 9 patchwork squares. Sew white squares to the patchwork squares, following the diagram. First sew a strip made up of pieces 2, 3, and 4. Next, a strip with pieces 5, 6, 7, 8, and 9. Then a strip with pieces 10, 11, 12, 13, 14, 15, and 16, then a strip with pieces 17, 18, 19, 20, and 21, and last, a strip with pieces 22, 23, and 24. Sew the strips together, placing pieces 1 and 3 diagonally opposite pieces 25 and 23.

Sew a strip of pink cotton to each edge of the patchwork square with 1/8" (.5 cm) seam allowance. Sew squares of printed cotton in the corners with 1/4" (1 cm) seam allowance. Sew on the edging strips, mitering the corners. Assemble and finish the pillow as for the cross stitch pillow. ∎

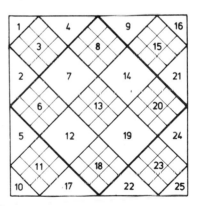

Patchwork Pillow Pattern

PILLOW WITH CORDED EDGE

~

• MATERIALS

3/4 yd (.6 m) white polished cotton fabric 45" (115 cm) wide, 1/4 yd (.3 m) white cotton brocade fabric 45" (115 cm) wide, thick white cotton yarn, 1-1/4 yds (1 m) white ribbon 1/2" (1.5 cm) wide, thread, pillow form 14" x 18" (35 cm x 45 cm). Kraft paper, piece of cardboard 3-1/2" (9 cm) square.

• INSTRUCTIONS

On paper, draw a rectangle 14" x 18" (35 cm x 45 cm). Draw diagonal lines from corner to corner to make 4 triangles. With the narrow triangle cut 2 pieces of polished cotton, adding 1/4" (1 cm) seam allowance. With the wide triangle, cut 2 pieces of brocade, adding 1/4" (1 cm) seam allowance. For the back, cut 2 pieces of polished cotton 8" x 18-3/4" (20.5 cm x 47 cm). All pieces are sewn with right sides together and with 1/4" (1 cm) seam allowances.

Sew the triangles together, alternating polished cotton with brocade, to form a rectangle. Sew the back pieces together along one long edge, leaving 12" (30 cm) open at the center of the seam. Stitch double hems along the seam allowances of the opening. Cut the ribbon into 4 equal pieces and sew them to the hems of the opening, 2 on each side. Sew the pillow front and back together around the outer edge. Trim corners and turn right side out.

Cut 3 strands of cotton yarn 11 yds (10 m) long. Fold the strands double and twist into a cord. Double the cord and twist again. Sew around the outer edge of the pillow by hand. Make 12 tassels, using the drawing as a guide. Wrap yarn around the cardboard 25 times. Remove from the cardboard. Wrap a strand of yarn around the tassel near the top, and cut at the bottom. Sew 3 tassels to each corner of the pillow. Insert the pillow form and tie the ribbons. ■

ROLL PILLOW

∾

• **FINISHED MEASUREMENTS**
24" (60 cm) long, 6" (15 cm) in diameter.

• **MATERIALS**
3/4 yd (.6 m) white cotton fabric 45" (115 cm) wide, 3/4 yd (.6 m) printed white cotton voile 45" (115 cm) wide, thread, pillow form 24" (60 cm) long and 6" (15 cm) in diameter. Kraft paper, compass.

• **INSTRUCTIONS**
With compass, draw a circle 6" (15 cm) in diameter on the paper. Use this pattern to cut 2 pieces of the cotton, adding 1/4" (1 cm) seam allowance. Cut a piece of cotton 19-1/2" x 24-3/4" (49 cm x 62 cm). From the voile, cut a piece

19-1/2" x 45" (49 cm x 115 cm), and 2 strips 2" x 20" (5 cm x 50 cm). All pieces are sewn with right sides together and 1/4" (1 cm) seam allowances.

Fold the cotton rectangle in half lengthwise and stitch the long edges, leaving 10" (25 cm) open at the center of the seam. Pin the circles in the ends and stitch. Turn right side out, insert the pillow form, and whipstitch the opening.

Fold the large piece of voile in half lengthwise and sew the long edges together. Turn right side out. Stitch narrow double hems around the ends of the tube. Fold the voile strips in half lengthwise. Sew the raw edges together around 3 sides, leaving an opening at the center of the long edge. Trim corners and turn right side out. Insert the covered pillow form into the voile tube, and tie the ends as shown in the photo. ∎

LACE-TRIMMED PILLOW

∾

• **FINISHED MEASUREMENTS**
20" (50 cm) square.

• **MATERIALS**
1 yd (.9 m) white polished cotton 45" (115 cm) wide, 5 yds (4.5 m) white lace 3-1/4" (8 cm) wide with 2 finished edges, white thread, 2 covered button forms 1-1/4" (3 cm) in diameter, 1 yd (.9 m) white ribbon 1/4" (1 cm) wide, pillow form 20" (50 cm) square, thread, kraft paper.

• **INSTRUCTIONS**
Make a paper pattern 20" (50 cm) square. Draw diagonal lines from

corner to corner and cut into triangles. Use one of the triangles as a pattern and cut 4 fabric triangles, adding 1/4" (1 cm) seam allowance and with the lower edge of the triangle on the crosswise grain of the fabric. For the back, cut 2 pieces 10-3/4" x 20-1/2" (27.5 cm x 52 cm). Cut 4 pieces of lace 14" (35 cm) long. Sew all pieces with right sides together and 1/2" (1 cm) seam allowance.

Pin one piece of lace across the long side of each triangle, 4-1/4" (11 cm) above the lower edge. Be sure the lace is positioned exactly the same on all triangles. Sew the lace in place, stitching 1/4" (1 cm) from each edge. Sew 2 triangles together, and continue until the 4 triangles are sewn together to form a square. Machine baste along one finished edge of the remaining piece of lace. Gather the lace to fit the top, allowing extra fullness at the corners. Pin the ruffle to the right side of the top, the gathered edge even with the edge of the top, and stitch.

Sew the 2 backing pieces together along one long edge, leaving 14" (35 cm) open at the center of the seam. Stitch double hems in the seam allowances of the opening. Place the backing and top together and stitch around the edges. Trim corners, turn right side out, and insert the pillow form. Cut the ribbon into 4 equal pieces and sew to the hemlines of the back opening. Cover the buttons with white fabric. Place one at the center of the top and the other directly below it on the back. Sew the buttons together through the pillow form. ■

PILLOW WITH SHIRRED BORDER

∽

- **FINISHED MEASUREMENTS**
17" (43 cm) square.

- **MATERIALS**
5/8 yd (.5 m) white cotton sateen 45" (115 cm) wide, printed white cotton voile 9-1/4" (24 cm) square, 2-1/4 yd (2 m) white cording 3/8" (1 cm) in diameter, 1-1/4 yds (1 m) white satin ribbon 1/4" (1 cm) wide, thread, pillow form 16" (40 cm) square, kraft paper.

- **INSTRUCTIONS**
Make a paper pattern for the front border. Draw a 17" (43 cm) square and draw diagonal lines across it from corner to corner to make 4 triangles.

Draw a square at the center, 8-3/4" (22 cm) on a side. Cut out one of the triangles, cut the triangular shape off this piece, and use the remaining piece as a border pattern. Cut 4 of the border pieces from the sateen, adding 1/4" (1 cm) seam allowance on all sides, and cut 2 pieces 9-1/2" x 17-1/2" (24.5 cm x 45 cm) for the back. Cut a 9-1/4" (24 cm) square. To assemble the pillow, sew all pieces with right sides together and with 1/4" (1 cm) seam allowances.

Sew the 4 border pieces together at the diagonal corners. Sew the voile square to the sateen square with both pieces right side up, using 1/8" (.5 cm) seam allowance. Sew the border to the square. Sew the 2 back pieces together along one long edge, leaving 14" (35 cm) open at the center of the seam. Stitch double hems along the seam allowances of the opening. Cut the ribbon into 4 equal pieces. Sew them to the hems of the opening, 2 on each side. ■

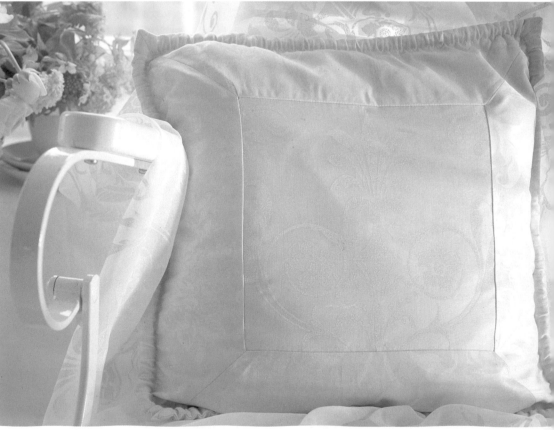

ROUND PILLOW WITH BOW

• **FINISHED MEASUREMENTS**

16-1/2" (42 cm) in diameter.

• **MATERIALS**

1 yd (.8 m) white polished cotton fabric 56" (140 cm) wide, 1/2 yd (.5 m) white cotton twill 45" (115 cm) wide for the bow, 3-1/2 yds (3 m) thin piping cord, thread, pillow form 16-1/4" (42 cm) in diameter. Kraft paper, compass.

• **INSTRUCTIONS**

On paper, draw a circle 16-1/2" (42 cm) in diameter with the compass. Use this pattern to cut the back piece from polished cotton, adding 1/4" (1 cm) seam allowance. Cut a strip of cotton 8-1/2" x 53-1/2" (21.5 cm x 134 cm) for the shirred front. For the edge panel, cut a strip 3-1/2" x 53-1/2" (9 cm x 134 cm), and for the piping, cut 2 strips 1-1/4" x 53-1/2" (3 cm x 134 cm). From the white twill, cut a strip 8-3/4" x 45" (22 cm x 115 cm), a strip 8-3/4" x 22" (22 cm x 55 cm), and a strip 6" x 7" (15 cm x 18 cm). All pieces are sewn with right sides together and with 1/4" (1 cm) seam allowances.

Fold a piping strip in half lengthwise, right side out, around a length of cord. Sew with a cording foot or zipper foot, stitching close to the cord. Make 2 lengths of piping this way. Pin the piping to each edge of the side panel strip with raw edges together and the stitching line of the piping on the seamline of the side panel. Stitch on the previous stitching lines. Sew the ends together to form a ring, turning the piping seam allowances to the inside.

Sew the ends of the front piece together. Sew one edge of this ring to the side panel strip so that the piping is between the side panel and the front piece. Sew the back to the side panel in the same way. Stitch a 1/2" (1.5 cm) hem along the remaining edge of the front. Turn the cover right side out and insert the pillow form. Insert a piece of cord in the hem of the front piece, draw it tight, and knot the cord.

To make the bow, fold the 22" (55 cm) twill strip in half lengthwise. Stitch the long edges, leaving an opening at the center of the seam. Fold so the seam is at center back, and sew across the ends. Trim corners, turn right side out, and stitch across the opening. Make the long strip the same way, but stitch diagonally across the ends. Fold the short strip in half lengthwise and sew just the long edges. Turn.

Make a double bow with the 2 longer pieces as shown in the photo. Wrap the short piece around the center of the bow and tack in place. Stitch to the pillow front over the opening. ■

BUILDING PILLOWS

~

- **FINISHED MEASUREMENTS**
16-1/2" (42 cm) square.

- **MATERIALS**
Small pieces of cotton fabric in the following colors: white, light gray, gray, black, light yellow, yellow, brown, rust, dark brown, green, dark green, pale turquoise, turquoise, blue, dark blue, and dark red. Thread in matching colors, tracing paper, dressmakers' carbon, glue stick. For each pillow, 1/2 yd (.4 m) cotton fabric in a coordinating color, 1 yd (.9 m) double fold bias tape 1/2" (1.5 cm) wide to match fabric, pillow form.

- **INSTRUCTIONS**
Cut one piece 17" (44 cm) square for each pillow front. Cut 2 pieces 17" x 9" (44 cm x 23 cm) for the back.

Enlarge the graph to actual size and draw it on tracing paper. Trace the pieces onto the fabrics, using the color key and the photos for guidance. Arrange the larger pieces on the pillow front first, and secure them with glue stick. Turn under 1/4" (1 cm) of any edges that will not be covered by other pieces. Edge-stitch the pieces in place. Follow the same procedure for the medium-sized pieces. Applique the very small pieces in place, stitching over the raw edges with a close, narrow zigzag stitch.

To assemble the pillows, first sew the back pieces together along one long edge, with right sides together and 1/2" (1.5 cm) seam allowance, leaving 8" (20 cm) open at the center. Stitch double hems along the seam allowances of the opening. Cut the bias tape into 4 equal pieces. Sew them to each side of the back opening, opposite each other in pairs. Stitch the front to the back with right sides together and 1/4" (1 cm) seam allowance around all edges. Trim the corners, turn right side out, and insert the pillow form. ■

Patterns for Building Pillows

Color Key

1	White	9	Dark Brown
2	Light Gray	10	Green
3	Gray	11	Dark Green
4	Black	12	Light Turquoise
5	Light Yellow	13	Turquoise
6	Yellow	14	Blue
7	Brown	15	Dark Blue
8	Rust	16	Dark Red

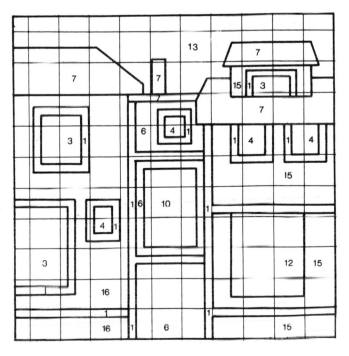

CHRISTMAS DOVE

✍

• **FINISHED MEASUREMENTS**
6-1/4" (16 cm) long.

• **MATERIALS**
1/4 yd (.2 m) white cotton fabric
45" (115 cm) wide, thread, dressmaker's carbon, loose-pack fiberfill,
2 buttons 3/16" (.5 cm) in diameter,
kraft paper.

• **INSTRUCTIONS**
Make a full-size paper pattern. Trace
onto fabric. Cut 2 body pieces, adding 1/4" (1 cm) seam allowance.

Sew the body pieces with right sides
together, leaving an opening along
the lower edge for turning. Clip
corners and turn the pieces right
side out. Stuff with fiberfill and
stitch across the openings.

Stitch the markings on the tail,
stitching all the way through.
Position the buttons, for eyes,
and sew them together through
the head. ■

**Christmas Dove Pattern,
shown actual size.**

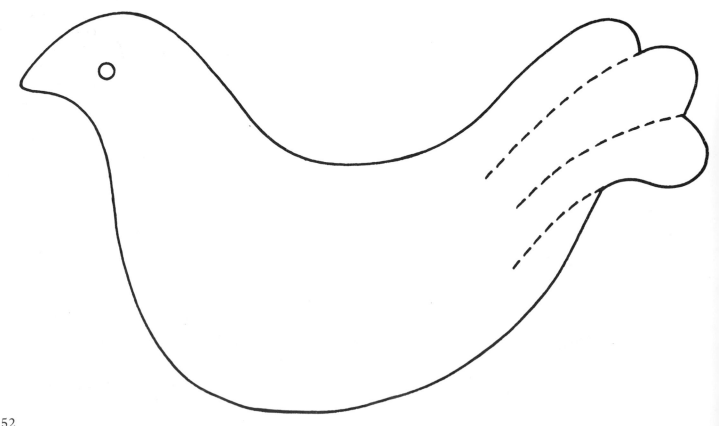

152

fabric with the triangles between them. Place the fiberfill batting on top of pieces. Sew around edges, leaving an opening on one side. Trim corners, turn right side out, and stitch across the opening. ■

CHRISTMAS BALL

s

• FINISHED MEASUREMENTS
3-1/4" (8 cm) in diameter.

• MATERIALS
6 pieces of fabric in coordinating red/white prints, loose-pack fiberfill, 12" (30 cm) red ribbon 1" (2.5 cm) wide, 16" (40 cm) thin red ribbon, tracing paper.

• INSTRUCTIONS
Draw a full-size pattern on tracing paper. Cut one piece from each fabric. Sew 3 pieces together twice to make 2 halves. Sew the 2 halves together, leaving an opening to stuff. Turn right side out, stuff, and stitch across the opening.

Make a bow with the wide ribbon and sew to top of ball. Fold the small ribbon double and sew ends to the ball around the bow. Hang the ball by the loop. ■

BREAD BASKET NAPKIN

s

• FINISHED MEASUREMENTS
24" (60 cm) square.

• MATERIALS
Red printed fabric, waffle white cotton fabric, fiberfill all 23" (58 cm) square, 3/8 yd (.3 m) red/white striped cotton fabric 45" (115 cm) wide. Basket 14" (35 cm) wide and 6-3/4" (17 cm) high with handle.

• INSTRUCTIONS
For the cloth, cut 56 pieces from striped fabric 2-3/4" (7 cm) square. Fold the squares double, right side out, to form small triangles and fold in half again to form smaller triangles. Pin the triangles to the red printed fabric with open edges of the triangles at the edge of the fabric. Each triangle should slightly overlap the previous triangle and be placed 1/4" (1 cm) from the edge of the red fabric (right side on right side) with folded open ends at the overlapping edges. Place 14 triangles on each side. Place the right side of the white fabric on the right side of the red

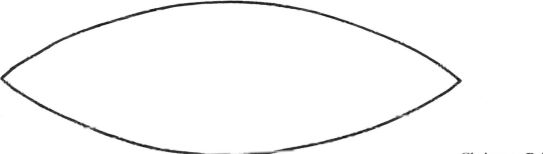

Christmas Ball Pattern, shown actual size.

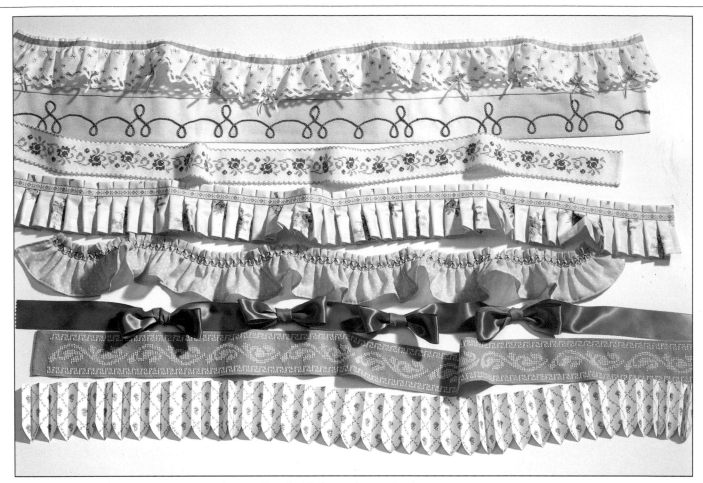

Attach a decorative edging to the front of a shelf, for a dressy look.

EYELET SHELF EDGING

∽

• **MATERIALS**

Embroidered eyelet with one finished edge, about 3-1/2" (9 cm) wide. Pink ribbon 1/8" (3 mm) wide. Pink ribbon 1/4" (1 cm) wide. Blue embroidery floss, pink thread.

• **INSTRUCTIONS**

Measure the length of the shelf, then cut edging 1-1/2 times that length. Cut the wide ribbon that length plus 3/4" (2 cm). From the thin ribbon, cut 5" (13 cm) lengths for bows, making one bow for each 5" (13 cm) of the edging. Accent the edging with blue stars, embroidered with 3 strands of floss. Thread narrow

ribbon through lower eyelets, leaving 1-1/2" (4 cm) at each end, and tack in place. Make bows with 3 loops and sew to lower edge at eyelets. Fold under the top edge and gather to the length of shelf allowing 1/4" (1 cm) at each end to turn under. Sew wide ribbon across the top. Fold the ends of the ribbon to the wrong side and sew in place.. ∎

CORDED EDGING

∽

• **MATERIALS**

A strip of blue cotton fabric 5" (12.5 cm) wide. Blue cord. Matching blue embroidery floss. Tracing paper, dressmakers' carbon.

Corded Edging Motif

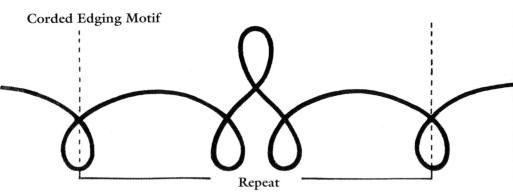

Repeat

• INSTRUCTIONS

Make a full-size drawing of the motif on tracing paper. Measure the length of the shelf, and cut fabric that length plus 1-1/4" (3 cm). Fold 1" (2.5 cm) of the upper edge to the wrong side, then fold back 1/4" (1 cm) to the right side and slip-stitch in place. Fold the lower edge and ends 3/4" (2 cm) to the wrong side and stitch. Use dressmakers' carbon to transfer the motif to the fabric, with the lower edge of the motif 1/2" (1.5 cm) from the lower edge of the fabric. Place the cord over the transfer lines and stitch in place with embroidery floss. ∎

ROSE EDGING

• MATERIALS

Aida band 2" (5 cm) wide with pink scalloped edges and 15 threads per inch (2.5 cm). Pink and green embroidery floss

• INSTRUCTIONS

Measure the length of the shelf, then cut edging that length plus 1-1/4" (3 cm). Make 5/8" (1.5 cm) double hems at the ends. Following the chart, embroider motifs along the strip, using 2 strands of floss over one thread for each stitch. ∎

PLEATED EDGING

᠗

• FINISHED MEASUREMENTS

3" (7.5 cm) wide.

• MATERIALS

A strip of printed cotton fabric 4-3/4" (12 cm) wide, embroidered ribbon 1/2" (1.5 cm) wide, thread.

• INSTRUCTIONS

Measure the length of the shelf and cut fabric twice this length. Stitch a 1/2" (1.5 cm) double hem at each end. Fold even pleats along the upper edge of the strip and press them in place along the top. Fold the pleated edge 1" (2.5 cm) to the wrong side. Stitch across the pleats, 3/4" (2 cm) below the folded edge. Stitch a 1/2" (1.5 cm) double hem across the lower edge. Place the ribbon 1/2" (1.5 cm) below the upper edge of the strip, and stitch it along both edges. ∎

SMOCKED EDGING

᠗

• FINISHED MEASUREMENTS

2-7/8" (7.25 cm) wide.

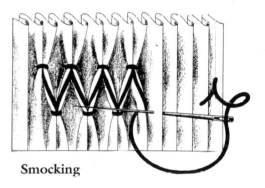

Smocking

• MATERIALS

A strip of polka dot fabric with 1/4" (1 cm) between dots, 6" (15 cm) wide. Blue embroidery floss.

• INSTRUCTIONS

Measure the length of the shelf. Cut fabric twice this length plus 4-1/4" (11 cm). Along the lower edge, stitch a 3/8" (1 cm) double hem. Along the upper edge, stitch a 1" (2.5 cm) hem, above a row of dots. Stitch a 3/8" (1 cm) double hem at each end. Using 3 strands of floss, smock a row of chevron stitches by following the sketch. Make each pleat 3 rows of dots high and 2 rows of dots wide. Smock 3/8" (1 cm) from the upper edge. (See smocking step by step, page 93.) ∎

Color Key

		DMC	Anchor
◤	Pink	956	54
⊠	Green	959	186

Rose Edging

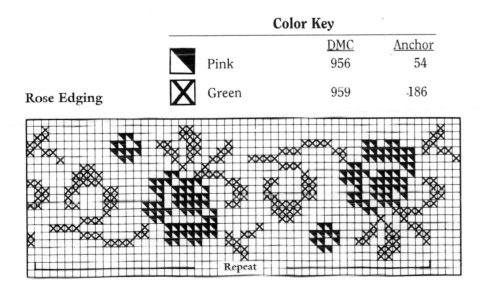

Repeat

BOW EDGING

*

• **MATERIALS**

Pink ribbon 1-1/2" (4 cm) wide.

• **INSTRUCTIONS**

Measure the length of the shelf.
Allow 12" (30 cm) for each bow and
7" (18 cm) between the bows. Tie
bows in the ribbon, and tack to the
shelf. ■

GREEK EDGING

*

• **MATERIALS**

Blue hardanger cloth strip 2-1/2"
(6 cm) wide with 25 threads per inch
(2.5 cm) and with finished edges.
White embroidery floss.

• **INSTRUCTIONS**

Measure the length of the shelf. Cut
cloth this length plus 1-1/4" (3 cm).
Stitch a 3/8" (1 cm) double hem at

Greek Edging

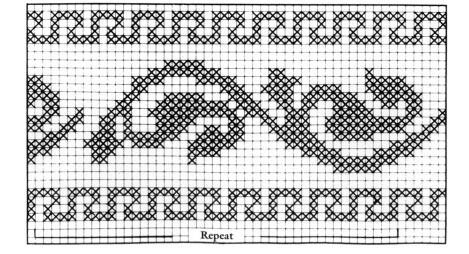

each end. Following the chart,
embroider the motif across the strip.
Use 2 strands of floss over 2 double
threads. Each motif is about 4"
(10 cm) wide. ■

PAPER EDGING

*

• **FINISHED MEASUREMENTS**

4" (10 cm) wide.

• **MATERIALS**

Flowered paper, ruler, craft knife,
double-sided tape.

• **INSTRUCTIONS**

Measure the length of the shelf. Cut
a paper strip 1-1/2 times this length
plus 3-1/4" (8 cm), and 4" (10 cm)
wide. On the wrong side of the
paper, mark every 1-1/4" (3 cm).
Fold the strip at the marks to form
accordion pleats. With the knife, cut
the scalloped edge. Stick tape to the
shelf edge, and stick the pleated strip
to it, adjusting the strip to fit. ■

FABRIC-COVERED FLOWER POT

*

• **MATERIALS**

2 identical plastic pots 7" (18 cm)
high and with 8-1/4" (21 cm) top
diameter. Fuchsia fabric with polka
dots 32" (80 cm) square. Orange
fabric with polka dots, about 5-1/2"
x 60" (14 cm x 150 cm). Matching
paint.

• **INSTRUCTIONS**

Paint the outside of 1 flower pot. Cut
a circle of fuchsia fabric 32" (80 cm)
in diameter. Place the unpainted pot
on the wrong side of fabric, fold the
fabric over the top, and insert second
pot in the first to hold the fabric in
place. Fold the orange fabric strip in
half lengthwise. Sew, using 1/4"
(1 cm) seam allowance and leaving
ends open. Turn right side out. Cut
the ends diagonally and tie around
top of pot as shown in photo. ■

MIRROR FRAME WITH FABRIC MAT

∽

• **FINISHED MEASUREMENTS**

14-1/2" x 20" (37 cm x 51 cm) and oval mirror 6-3/4" x 10-3/4" (17 cm x 27 cm).

• **MATERIALS**

An oval mirror, frame, paint. 1 yd. (.8 m) fuchsia fabric with polka dots 45" (115 cm) wide. 2 pieces of cardboard 14" x 19-1/2" (35.5 cm x 49.5 cm). White glue.

• **INSTRUCTIONS**

For the front, center the mirror on 1 piece of cardboard. Draw the outline and cut out the oval. Cut 2 pieces of fabric 8-3/4" x 22" (22 cm x 55 cm) and 2 pieces 8-3/4" x 30" (22 cm x 75 cm). Using 1/2" (1 cm) seam allowance, sew ends of 2 long strips to a long edge of one short strip, one at each end. Sew the other ends of the 2 long strips to the other short strip in the same way to form a hollow rectangle 22" x 45-1/2" (55 cm x 115 cm).

Cover the cardboard front with the fabric rectangle. Gather the edges, turn to inside, and glue in place. Glue the other piece of fabric to the second piece of cardboard. Glue the back to the front with fabric to the outside. Glue the mirror in place. Paint the frame and insert the mat and mirror. ∎

COILED LAUNDRY BASKET

~

• FINISHED MEASUREMENTS

15" (38 cm) high and 15" (38 cm) in diameter.

• MATERIALS

Cotton fabric in 3 different prints, 2-3/4 yds (2.5 m) of each, 45" (115 cm) wide. About 28 yds (25 m) rope, 1" (3 cm) in diameter, thread, tape.

• INSTRUCTIONS

Cut or tear each piece of fabric on the crosswise grain into strips 2-3/4" (7 cm) wide. Cut the fabric strips to different lengths to give the basket more variety. Wrap the ends of the rope tightly with tape to prevent unraveling. Working on a table, turn the end of a fabric strip 1/2" (1.5 cm) to the wrong side and wrap the strip around 4" (10 cm) of the rope. Wind the rope into a tight coil to begin the bottom of the basket. At the beginning of the second round, then every 4" (10 cm), double the fabric strip and knot it around the previous row as shown in the drawing. At the end of each strip, tape the strip around the rope to secure it, and cover the tape with the new strip. Continue this way until the diameter of the coil is 15" (38 cm).

Start the sides of the basket by placing the next round above the outer round of the bottom coil. Continue until the basket is about 13-1/2" (34 cm) high. Make the handles on the next 2 rounds: on the next round leave 2 unknotted spaces of 5" (12 cm) on opposite sides of the basket. On the following round, wrap strips around both ropes in those places to form the handles. End the last round with a knot. Cut the rope and cover the end by wrapping a fabric strip around it together with the rope below it. Stitch the end in place. ■

Every 4" tie the coil to the previous row.

The Finished Basket

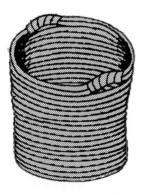

Beribboned Lampshade

⌘

• Materials

Cotton muslin, assorted wide ribbons, 1 length of narrow ribbon, a lamp with shade.

• Instructions

Using the original lampshade as a model, make a paper pattern. Draw around the lower opening of the shade and cut the circle from the paper. Repeat for the upper opening of the shade. Measure the height of the shade. Cut a piece of muslin the same width as the height of the shade plus 1/8" (.5 cm) top and bottom, and the length of the lower opening circumference plus 1/4" (1 cm) seam allowance at each end.

Overlap ends and sew in a cylinder. Remove the original shade from the metal form and replace with the muslin. Gather the top to fit over the form and stitch in place. Sew ribbons to the muslin, pleating and gathering as shown in the photo. Begin at the bottom, overlapping lower edge of the shade by 1/4" (1 cm). Overlap rounds of ribbon. End 1/4" (1 cm) above the top. Tie the narrow ribbon around the shade just below the top, and tie a bow. ■

Subject Index

Applique, Hungarian, 63; instructions, 64

Appliques, 16 (il)

Backings, tear-away, 12

Battings, 12

Carbon, dressmaker's, 12

Corners, 13

Cutters, rotary, 10; il. 11

Cutting mats, 10; il. 11

Cutting mats, 10; il. 11

Edgestitching, 16

Fabrics, decorator, 8; fashion, 9; natural fiber, 8; selection of, 8

Fray preventers, liquid, 12

Gathering, 17 (il)

Glues, fabric, 12; sticks, 12; white craft, 12

Grain, how to straighten, 12

Hems, 16

Interfacings, 12

Knives, craft, 12; il. 11

Measuring equipment, 10

Pattern drafting material, non-woven, 12

Pins, 10

Point turners, 10; il. 11

Pompons, instructions for, 142

Pressing, 13

Quilting, 17

Scissors, 10

Seam rippers, 12; il. 11

Seams, curved, 13

Sergers, 9

Sewing machines, 9

Smocking, English, instructions for, 93

Stenciling, 17

Stitch lengths, 13

Stuffings, 12

Tailor's knots, 13 (il)

Topstitching, 16

Transfer webs, paper-backed, 12

Zippers, 15-16

Index of Projects

Baby blanket, 128

Baby organizer, 128

Baby rug, 128

Basket, coiled laundry, 158; decorated, 80

Bed skirt, 104

Bedspread, holstein, 116; striped, 100, 111

Blanket, winter, 112

Boxes, fabric-covered, 24

Bread basket napkin, 153

Chair cover, laced backs, 95; striped, 60; overstuffed, 56; tied, 40

Chair cushion, checked, 35; pique, 105; ruffled, 78

Christmas ball, 153

Christmas dove, 152

Comforter cover, log cabin, 120

Crib blanket cover, patchwork, 124

Crib quilt, woven, 131

Curtain tieback, farm scene, 118

Curtains, bedroom, ruffled, 102; checked, 36; kitchen, 77; kitchen decorative bands, 88; kitchen puffy, 93; scalloped, 48

Cushions, covered, 41

Duck, patchwork, 20

Duvet cover, ruffled, 108

Flower pot, fabric-covered, 156

Guest book, 90

Hassock, 34

Jar covers, 85

Jar tops, fringed, 80

Lampshade, beribboned, 159; checked, 31

Mirror frame, 157

Napkins, 88; bordered, 26; fringed, 37

Oven mitt, 79

Picture frames, ruffled, 96

Picture hanger, 44

Picture mat, checked, 34; floral, 25

Pillow, black and white appliqued, 65; bouquet, 136; building, 150; corded edge, 146; crisscrossed, 36; cross stitch center, 138; floral, 23; folded, 144; lace-trimmed, 147; linen, 144; painted flowers, 134; patchwork, 145; pompon, 142; red bouquet, 143; red bow, 143; roll, 147; round ruffled, 136; round with bow, 149; shirred border, 148; stenciled, 100; striped, 23; tied, 143; tied corners, 136; white bouquet, 145; with bow, 134

Pillow cover, 90

Pillowcase, eyelet-trimmed, 108; patchwork, 124; striped, 100, 111

Pincushion, woven, 131

Potholder, stenciled, 74

Potpourris, pocket, 85

Quilt, buttoned, 50

Recipe folder, 76

Screen, folding, 43

Shelf edging, bow, 156; corded, 154; eyelet, 154; Greek, 156; paper, 156; pleated, 155; rose, 155; ruffled, 74; smocked, 93, 155

Soft sculpture, teapot, 27

Table skirt, pleated, 111

Tablecloth, bordered, 26; crisscrossed, 77

Tray cloth, stenciled, 51

Vase, fabric-covered, 31, 41

Wreath, potpourri, 85; braided fabric, 44